# Scales on Censorship

# Scales on Censorship

## Real Life Lessons from *School Library Journal*

By Pat R. Scales

*Edited by School Library Journal's*
Rebecca T. Miller and Barbara A. Genco

ROWMAN & LITTLEFIELD
*Lanham • Boulder • New York • London*

Published by Rowman & Littlefield
A wholly owned subsidiary of The Rowman & Littlefield Publishing Group, Inc.
4501 Forbes Boulevard, Suite 200, Lanham, Maryland 20706
www.rowman.com

Unit A, Whitacre Mews, 26-34 Stannary Street, London SE11 4AB

Cover Design by Mark Tuchman and Design layout by Josephine Marc-Anthony

British Library Cataloguing in Publication Information Available

**Library of Congress Cataloging-in-Publication Data**

Library of Congress Control Number: 2015934398

ISBN 978-1-4422-5063-5

*For Alonda Rollison, Sarah Smeal, and Jane Wassynger,*
*English Teachers, Colleagues, and Friends.*

*You are my Idols.*

# Contents

# *Preface*

Pat Scales has been a passionate advocate for intellectual freedom long before she launched the "Scales on Censorship" column with *School Library Journal* in 2006. Decades of experience as a school librarian informs her ongoing work on these important and often volatile issues, as did her tenure in leadership roles on the American Library Association's Intellectual Freedom Committee and at the Freedom To Read Foundation. It also earned her a place among the inaugural list of *Library Journal's* Movers & Shakers in 2002. Since her first column for *SLJ* she has been in an ongoing conversation of sorts with librarians, teachers, and parents—a much needed conversation. This collection of the wide-ranging questions from readers and Scales' informative answers are gathered in broad thematic groups to help readers explore the all-too daily reality of confronting efforts to censor, ban, or otherwise limit open and ready access to materials in our schools and libraries. Her passionate, unwavering voice provides valuable strategic and tactical approaches to censorship, fine-tuned insight into individual books often challenged, and critical moral support for managing trying conversations. Scales is focused throughout on fostering a culture that embraces and understands the importance of intellectual freedom, and the tools to make it a reality every day in our libraries, schools, and communities. Learn from her to build a background in the ethics involved in defending intellectual freedom and lean on her for insights into real-life situations. Scales on censorship is an essential ally in the ongoing fight.

—*Rebecca T. Miller*

# Introduction

## Up to the Challenge

### By Pat Scales

*"Students do not shed their constitutional rights to freedom of speech or expression at the schoolhouse gate."*

Supreme Court Justice Abe Fortas
*Tinker* v. *Des Moines*, 1969

I became interested in matters related to intellectual freedom in the early 1970s. At that time newspapers and professional journals reported that people were challenging and banning *Sylvester and the Magic Pebble* by William Steig because of the "pig" policemen, and that *Portnoy's Complaint* by Phillip Roth was imprisoned in the basement of the Memphis Public Library because a mother was outraged that her 15-year-old boy had borrowed the book. In those days it was very hard to track censorship cases. Now the digital age makes it much easier for the American Library Association's Office for Intellectual Freedom and the National Coalition Against Censorship to monitor such attempts to abridge free speech. Among the issues that these organizations deal with are book challenges in public and school libraries as well as issues with content taught in the classroom, labeling, Internet filtering, privacy, student journalism and art, and students' rights to openly debate issues that may be deemed "controversial" or "inappropriate" by some people.

During Occupy Wall Street, I heard a high school teacher say, "I told my students not to pay any attention to the news about this event because most of those people didn't have any idea of what they were protesting." It's probably true that some of the protesters didn't have a clue why they were there, but over the course of weeks of occupation I suspect that they learned. The same could be said for some who marched with the Suffragettes and with Martin Luther King, Jr. on their drives to gain equal rights for women and African Americans. Instead of assuming that protesters are ignorant to their causes, it's much better to admire them for practicing their "right to peaceably assemble," a basic tenet of the First Amendment. This teacher squandered a teachable moment and should have engaged her students in a healthy debate about the issues. She might have even sent them to the library to research the pros and cons of the protest, and asked them to explain the slogan, "We are the 99%." Why was the teacher so eager to share her views without asking students to express theirs? Now there is a movement in some states to rewrite the high school American History curriculum to ban any reference to "civil discourse." Yet it's "civil discourse" that shaped America's history and created the democracy in which we live.

In 1966 when the principal of East High School in Des Moines, Iowa, suspended Mary Beth Tinker and fellow classmates for wearing black armbands in protest of the war in Vietnam, he assumed that he had the right to suppress students' views. A three-year court battle ended in 1969 when the Supreme Court upheld the students' right to free expression and issued a warning to schools that they couldn't deny students the right to speak simply because they wanted to avoid controversy (*Tinker* v. *Des Moines Independent Community School District*). Today there are new threats to students' free speech rights as school officials develop policies that govern what students can say in email and on social media websites. There are even reports that some schools punish students for "inappropriate" online activity conducted outside of school. Mary Beth Tinker believes that her victory in 1969 is applicable to students in the "digital age," and she is crisscrossing the nation and speaking with students about their First Amendment rights in and out of school.

Almost a decade after the *Tinker* case, the school board in Levittown, New York, removed 11 books from the high school library because board members felt the works were "anti-American, anti-Semitic, anti-Christian, and just plain filthy." Stephen Pico, a high school student, fought diligently to get the books returned to their rightful place on the shelves in the school library.

What followed was a lengthy court battle that came to a close in 1982 when the Supreme Court ruled that a school board couldn't remove books from a school library simply because they disagree with the ideas expressed in the books (*Board of Education, Island Trees Union Free School District* v. *Pico*).

A more recent court case occurred in Cedarville, Arkansas, when parents of a fourth-grader challenged the decision by school officials requiring students to have written parental permission to read the Harry Potter books. The parents felt such requirement would label their child "evil" in the eyes of classmates whose parents objected to the books. The court ruled against the school administration, and the books were returned to the open shelves.

While most challenges to students' First Amendment rights don't end up in court, other practices that limit and deny access to books and information students' need are raising concerns among free speech advocates. One such practice is labeling and shelving books by reading level. The political emphasis on student achievement has caused school districts to buy into computerized reading programs like Accelerated Reader (AR) that test students on every book they read. Some schools actually restrict students to books on their level, and now public libraries are succumbing to the pressure to label books so that patrons may easily access the books they need for school. This is a serious threat to traditional reader guidance practices and contradicts the very purpose of education—to encourage students to stretch and grow their minds by reading widely and by engaging in open inquiry.

Labeling books and materials for objectionable content is one of the most pervasive issues in school and public libraries today. There are websites like Common Sense Media, Facts on Fiction, and the Literate Mother that assign "warnings" about hot button issues like sex and sexuality, violence, language, and substance use and abuse. Some librarians feel these sites protect them from potential challenges. But there are documented cases that these websites have actually resulted in the removal of books from libraries. A close examination of these websites reveals that the "reviewers" are simply working from a checklist. There is no real knowledge of the literature, and some of the information provided is wrong. For example, Facts on Fiction states that *To Kill a Mockingbird* by Harper Lee won the Caldecott Medal, an award given to illustrations in a children's book. Defendants of such sites claim that librarians should read multiple reviews when selecting books and materials. This is very true, but the question remains: Are these websites really providing reviews?

Book censorship is, and probably always will be, a big issue for school and public libraries. Novels that have been on library shelves for years are often challenged when movie adaptations are released. This occurred with *The Perks of Being a Wallflower* by Stephen Chbosky and *The Golden Compass* by Philip Pullman. Political battles over issues such as gay marriage bring challenges to books such as *And Tango Makes Three* by Justin Richardson and Peter Parnell and *The Miseducation of Cameron Post* by Emily M. Danforth. Organized groups are evangelical in their drive to *sanitize* what children and young adults read, view, and study. It's difficult to fight these groups because they have money, and can easily gain an audience through local and national media and social websites. Librarians and teachers feel threatened and frightened because school and public library boards too often react to the loudest and most relentless voices.

A lot has happened in the years since Mary Beth Tinker and Stephen Pico courageously fought and won their free speech battles. The current Supreme Court is more conservative, causing some free speech experts to speculate whether Tinker and Pico could be successful in the court system today. The post September 11 hysteria has managed to convince some politicians, law enforcement, and school administrators that less speech is the only way to keep America and schools safe. Most censorship cases are born out of such fear, but knowledge is always safer than ignorance.

The good news is that the American Library Association continues to mobilize its effort to make the public and professional community conscious of free speech issues as they develop. No one denies that it takes courage to face the censor, but there are people and organizations throughout the nation that take a personal and professional stance to protect intellectual freedom for all Americans, including children and young adults. The First Amendment is a gift from our forefathers, and it's important that we pay it forward.

# 1

# Collection Development and Censorship

## Policies, pre-censorship, selection, weeding, reconsideration, and more

Questions from the field illustrate the many faces of censorship and the need for consisentent policy-based process and ongoing education about the ethics involved in maintaining a vital collection. The educational component is especially critical and sensitive when it comes to administrators, who can experience pressure on many fronts and be unprepared to respond. Scales' message is a steady and strong one: have a policy and a process for handling challenges, communicate it effectively and proactively, and embrace opportunities to engage in deeper conversations about the content of the books in question. Also critical is for librarians themselves to stay up to speed on the books in hand and to leave personal biases at the door when it comes to the collections they manage. Censorship, some of these entries indicate, does not always begin outside the library, so remaining alert to the chilling effect of prior challenges is essential. The key, Scales asserts, is process, process, process. —R. T. M.

I'm a collection development librarian for a very large public library. It's our job to order books for the entire system. One of the bookmobile librarians is extremely conservative and doesn't want us to send the "Diary of a Wimpy Kid" (Abrams) series or the "Captain Underpants" (Scholastic) series to her bookmobile. She says she's read that these books have been banned in some libraries, and she can't defend them. Circulation data reveals the popularity of these books, but we can't seem to convince her. *April 2014*

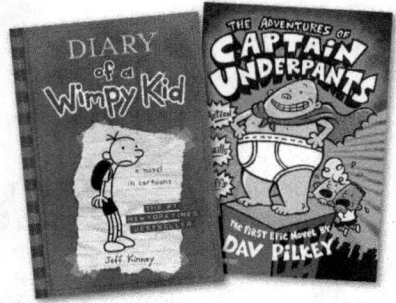

The first thing this librarian needs to understand is that the bookmobile doesn't belong to her. It belongs to the public, including children. These are extremely popular books among young readers, and the readers need access to the books, whether in the children's room of the main library or on the shelves of a bookmobile. It's true that these series have been challenged, but they also have been successfully defended. Present the situation to the library director. It may be time to review the library's collection development and circulation policies. I hope these policies include a procedure for dealing with challenged materials. The bookmobile librarian must understand that it's not her job to judge what patrons are reading, and she mustn't let her personal views affect her professional services. She may need reassurance that she won't have to face challenges alone.

80 ◎ ʚ

I'm an elementary school librarian. Recently, our principal asked me to remove Amy Ignatow's entire *The Popularity Papers* (Amulet) from our collection after a parent complained about it. Our girls—and even some of the boys—really love these books. The fact that one of its main characters has two dads has never been an issue until the parent complained. When I asked our principal if he wanted me to remove the series because of the gay parents, he replied, "Yes, we can't support that." I haven't removed the books. What should I do? *April 2013*

Does your district have a Materials Reconsideration Policy that deals with specific challenges? If it does, review the policy with your principal and the parent. Let them know that following a proper procedure is the most professional way of handling a challenge. The courts have already said that school administrators can't pull a library book based on their "personal opinion or bias." Point to the case in Davis County, UT, where the school district removed Patricia Polacco's *In Our Mothers' House* (Philomel, 2009) from its shelves. Parents who wanted their kids to have access to the book sued the district. The school board has reinstated the book, but the court case isn't settled. If you don't have a policy, now is the time to develop one.

ℬ ◎ ℭ

**I just read a review of Lois Lowry's *Son* (Houghton Mifflin, 2012), and it sounds intriguing. Years ago, *The Giver* (Houghton Mifflin, 1993) was challenged in our middle school. The school district's reconsideration committee dealt with the challenge and recommended that the novel be retained. I haven't had any further problems with *The Giver*, but I'm afraid if I purchase *Son*, I may have problems. What should I do?** *January 2013*
Buy the book! Just because you had one challenge to *The Giver* doesn't mean that you'll have further problems with it, or with *Son*. If you do, it should be handled the same way as the initial challenge. Fans of *The Giver* will flock to *Son*, and you should give them that chance. And take the time to read it yourself. That's your best defense should a problem arise.

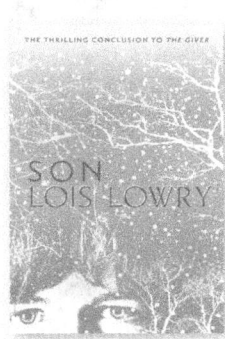

ℬ ◎ ℭ

**My middle school principal has warned me not to automatically order Newbery-winning books, because some of them have been challenged in our school. I feel that we need these prize-winning titles. Please advise.** *January 2013*
I don't know what Newbery books have been challenged in your school, but I could probably guess based on previous challenges. Make sure that your principal understands that the Newbery Medal is awarded to the author of "the most distinguished contribution to American Literature for children" published in the previous year. Children are defined as "persons of ages up to and including fourteen"—which clearly includes middle schoolers. Committee members consider the literary merit of books, and if they're doing their job, they don't focus on any possible controversy.

It sounds as if the principal is caving in to a few parents. Inform him that the majority of parents want their kids to read books that have literary merit, like the

Newbery winners. Talk with the language arts faculty and ask them to support your decision to include these titles in the collection. I bet they actually use them in their curriculum, and they may need your support as well. Let the principal know that if any parents complain about the titles, you'll handle it. I bet he'll take you up on that. He just wants them off his back.

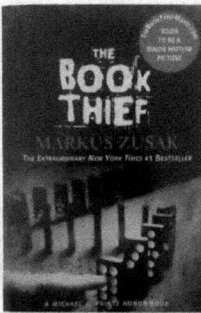

৪০ ◎ ୦୨

One of our social studies teachers requires her eighth graders to read a book of their choice about the Holocaust. After one of them chose Markus Zusak's *The Book Thief* (Knopf, 2006), she got a complaint from his mother, who told her that web site theliteratemother.org had recommended the book for older teens because of its language and violence. Now our principal wants me to remove it from our collection. When I explained that the parent needed to file a formal complaint and then the case would go before a reconsideration committee, he told me to skip that step. What should I do? *September 2012*

Sites that rate books are popping up everywhere, and they're causing librarians a lot of grief. I visited The Literate Mother website and discovered that it's using the same criteria as Common Sense Media. I wouldn't call anyone "literate" who takes words and scenes out of context like these sites do. If you do your homework, you'll find that none of these sites use professional reviewers. It's also not uncommon for them to take a simple kiss out of context and then point out that a book has sexual content. Remind your principal that students should be offered choices, and any book set during the Holocaust is bound to contain violence. This is a case in which a teacher is expected to teach, but a parent, and even the principal, doesn't want students to learn. Stick to your guns. It sounds as if your district has a formal process for dealing with book challenges, and you should stick to that, too.

৪০ ◎ ୦୨

Our district has had a rash of book challenges this year, and now the school board wants to narrow our selection policy. I don't have time to read every title I order for our library, but I feel accountable for what I select. I need help! *July 2012*

An organized group may be instigating these challenges. It sounds as if the school board doesn't have the courage to let parents know that what a child reads should be between the parent and child. And what about parents who want their kids to read widely and to learn about various cultures and lifestyles? Perhaps some of them will speak up on your behalf. Ask the school board if librarians can help create the new policy. Make sure that everyone understands that you have an obligation to serve all of your students, not just conservative ones. Hang tough. This may blow over.

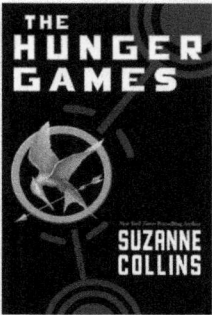

ℰℴ ◎ ℭℛ

Our fourth and fifth graders (and a few third graders) have been asking for *The Hunger Games* (Scholastic, 2008). I love the novel, but it's not in our elementary school's library collection because it's a YA book. I think my students would enjoy reading it when they're a bit older. I need your advice. *May 2012*

Elementary school students aren't the novel's intended audience. I have no doubt that some of your students are reading *The Hunger Games* because the movie is so hot right now. They're also attracted to the book because many older siblings are reading it. Don't worry. You aren't censoring. It's wise to base your purchasing decisions on the reviews you've read. A librarian has to make book-selection calls all the time, and reviews serve as our professional guidance tools.

One word of advice: I wouldn't tell your students that they're too young to read the novel. Instead, I'd say, "I've read *The Hunger Games*, and I think it's exciting, but there's not enough money in our budget to buy it. If you decide to read the story, I'd love to hear what you have to say about it." If a parent asks you about *The Hunger Games*, I'd tell them it's recommended for older readers.

ℰℴ ◎ ℭℛ

A group of parents recently visited our private school and demanded to know if the library had any gay and lesbian books. We have *And Tango Makes Three* (Simon & Schuster, 2005) in the elementary school library, and *Annie on*

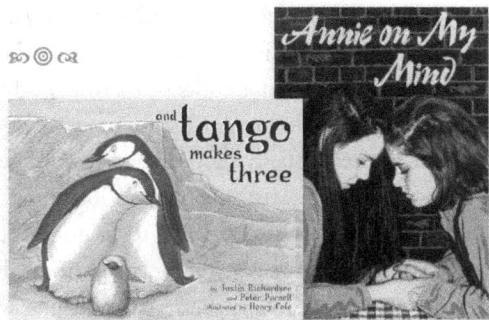

*My Mind* (Farrar Straus & Giroux, 1982) in the middle and high school library. The parents haven't filed a formal challenge, but they assured me they would if I didn't remove those titles. What should I do? *May 2012*

I suspect that you're in a fairly conservative community or you probably wouldn't have this problem. Many private schools have a narrow mission statement to accommodate the families they want to attract. Don't give in to those parents. Instead, let them file a challenge. I hope your school has a selection policy you can use to defend the titles. If not, now's the perfect time to develop one. I'd suggest that you look at similar independent schools' mission statements and selection policies as you create or tweak your own.

ဆ ◎ ଔ

Our school district has a materials review policy and a reconsideration form that we use when a challenge occurs. I sometimes think that the form actually encourages more challenges. Should we try to talk to parents before we offer the form? *November 2011*

Good conversation is always a good idea. Sometimes parents just want to be heard. Often, they haven't read the book, and once they understand its general themes they'll drop the complaint. On the other hand, if the conversation doesn't go anywhere, I'd simply say, "You need to complete this form so that a committee can consider your complaint." Make sure that the parent understands how important it is to complete the entire form. Librarians should view the reconsideration form as a tool for resolution.

ဆ ◎ ଔ

What happens to challenged books after they've been removed from a library collection? Are they ever returned to the collection? Or are they destroyed? *May 2011*

It depends on the library and its board of trustees. Sometimes, books that have been removed from a collection are stored in the library director's office or in a back room. Unfortunately, sometimes they are actually destroyed. Yes, removed books may eventually be returned to the shelves. Don't lose hope: library boards change, small-interest groups can lose their momentum, and public attitudes toward certain topics can shift. It's a good idea for a library board, under the direction of the library director, to periodically review its collection development policy, including its procedures for dealing with challenged materials.

Paul Monette's *Borrowed Time: An AIDS Memoir* (Harcourt Brace Jovanovich, 1988) was recently challenged in one of our middle schools. Now, the director of schools wants to amend our reconsideration policy to include the following provisions: (1) An emergency book-removal clause, which would give him the authority to remove books until the reconsideration committee convenes, if he thinks the books aren't worthy. Currently, challenged materials remain in the collection pending the committee's final decision. (2) A disruption clause, which would let him remove books that he feels are causing a disturbance, until the committee determines the ultimate fate of the books. (3) A revised schedule that would reduce—from 15 days to 48 hours—the amount of time that the reconsideration committee has to convene after a formal challenge has been made. Is it illegal for him to make these policy changes? By the way, he has the board of trustees' full support. *May 2011*

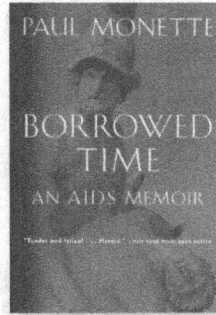

First of all, *Borrowed Time* is an adult book, and it's tough to defend its place in a middle school collection. I doubt the reconsideration committee will support keeping this particular title in the collection. That said, let's deal with the issues related to the proposed policy changes. It isn't illegal for the director of schools to change the reconsideration policy. But your school officials may find themselves up to their necks in quicksand if they attempt to enforce his proposed changes. For starters, under *Board of Education* v. *Pico*, 457 U.S. 853 (1982), the proposed emergency book-removal clause can be challenged. The Supreme Court's plurality opinion prohibits school officials from removing school library books based on their disagreement with the ideas expressed in those books. The proposed disruption clause is a weak attempt to apply *Hazelwood School District* v. *Kuhlmeier*, 484 U.S. 267 (1988) to Pico. Hazelwood grants school officials control over decisions related to the school curriculum (such as which novels can be used in English classes), but draws a distinction between curricular and non-curricular speech restrictions. Since students use libraries at will, they should expect greater free speech rights in a library setting. Finally, it's not a good idea to rush into forming a re-consideration committee. You'll want to make sure that its members represent the entire school community. Many school districts appoint a committee at the beginning of each new school year, so that it's in place when it's needed.

ഔ ◎ ഇ

In response to a librarian who asked about an employee who wouldn't let an 11-year-old check out a YA book, you once suggested, "Perhaps your library needs to offer some type of 'parent approved' card that lets kids access your entire collection." Doesn't that go against letting kids have free access to information? I thought that libraries should allow children to use the entire collection. *May 2011*

You're absolutely right: children should have access to all of the library's information, and I should have firmly stated that. Unfortunately, there are many public libraries that don't allow children to have free access to the entire collection. We should be equally concerned about a related problem: some libraries don't allow young adults in their children's rooms. A public library is a place for "free and unrestricted access" of information for all. Thank you for reminding me of that.

ℬ ◎ ℛ

I'm a school librarian in Texas. Because of budget cuts, I probably won't have a job next year. If that's the case, my principal plans to ask the PTA for volunteers to run the library. In the meantime, he wants me to "weed" any books that might be controversial, because he doesn't want future volunteers to face any censorship issues. Am I doomed if I refuse? *May 2011*

DO NOT WEED THE BOOKS. What do you have to lose? If you don't have a job, he can't fire you. If you still have a job there next year (let's hope), then you'll still have the materials you need to serve the students and their learning needs. If the principal approaches you again about this issue, simply tell him that "controversial" can't be defined and the task is impossible. Then, remind him that school librarians are necessary partners in students' educations.

ℬ ◎ ℛ

I learned in library school that you should never allow personal biases to interfere with decisions about collection development. Every year, our fifth-grade teachers teach a unit on the American Revolution. One of them doesn't think we have enough books in the library on the topic and she has requested that I buy a few more. But I have a personal problem with books that contain information about guns and violence. I just can't bring myself to buy them. Help! *November 2010*

You can't teach a unit on the American Revolution with-out the blood-and-guts part, and that includes information about guns and all sorts of crude weapons. The students can handle it. The question is, can you? The purpose of a school library is to expand students' knowledge and curiosity. Is the teacher recommending Russell Freedman's *Lafayette and the American Revolution* (Holiday House, 2010) and *Washington at Valley Forge* (Holiday House, 2008)? Freedman doesn't sugarcoat the truth.

If you give his works a chance, they may change your mind about children's books that deal with our nation's history, which, of course, includes war. You have to come to grips with this issue—or realize that you're in the wrong profession.

ℬ ◎ ☾

**An African-American parent has challenged Aaron Reynolds's *Metal Man* (Charlesbridge, 2008), citing its negative portrayal of African-American families and inappropriate dialect. Can you suggest some ways to approach this challenge?** *January 2010*

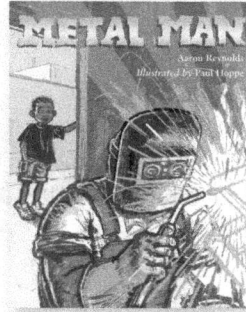

Do you have a materials selection policy? If you have one, then it's your best defense. If not, take this opportunity to create a policy that addresses how to deal with challenged materials. Sometimes parents need guidance in understanding a book's themes. Invite the parent to visit the library and watch you discuss the book with a group of elementary school students. Read the story exactly as it's written, and then read it again using Standard English. Ask kids how Standard English changes the text's poetic cadence. Discuss how each culture and region has its own colloquialisms and dialects. Stress that there's an "urban" language and a "rural" language. Kids will understand these concepts, and you may be surprised: their comments may change the parent's perception of the book.

ℬ ◎ ☾

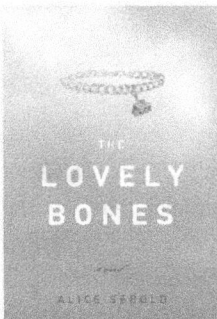

**We're having an interesting debate about whether to include Alice Sebold's *The Lovely Bones* (Little, Brown, 2002) in a middle school library. The debate became heated when someone suggested that they'd include the book, but require students to obtain parental permission to read it. That seems like a perfect solution, but is it a form of censorship?** *March 2010*

Please, examine your selection policy regarding purchasing adult materials for the middle school library. Just because a student asks for a book doesn't mean you have to rush out and purchase it. *The Lovely Bones* was published and reviewed as an adult book. Its point of view is too tough for most middle school kids to grasp. Don't forget that we have responsibility for reader guidance. There's nothing wrong with telling students, "No, we don't have that book, but we do have a similar book"—and then lead them to it. I can guarantee you that that will satisfy your readers. And yes, requiring parental permission is a form of censorship. In fact, in the case *Counts* v. *Cedarville School District*, a U.S. District Court has already ruled that a library can't require parental permission to check out a book.

80 ◎ ◑

A 10th-grade English teacher received an advanced reader's copy of a novel, and she'd like me to purchase it when it's available. While thumbing through her copy, I spotted the F-word on one of its pages. Now I'm worried about buying the book for our school library. What would you suggest? *January 2009*

You first need to read the entire book. Right now, you're doing what many censors do—taking a word or phrase out of context. I hope the teacher has read the entire novel, since she's so eager for you to add it to your collection. If she hasn't, encourage her to finish the book. After you've both had a chance to consider its literary merits, then you can have an informed and thoughtful discussion. But before you read the book, be honest with yourself. Because of the F-word, will you be searching for a flaw in the book so you can justify not purchasing it? If that's the case, then it's already doomed. On the other hand, suppose you read the book and discover it doesn't have much merit. Then you need to ask yourself two things: Is the novel comparable in literary quality to most of the others in our collection? Will the story appeal to students? If the answer to both questions is "yes," then you should purchase it. By the way, I bet there are already a number of excellent works of literature in your collection that contain the F-word.

80 ◎ ◑

A parent of one of our eighth graders came into the library and began pulling books off our shelves. She ended up stacking 15 books on the circulation desk—including *The Giver, The Chocolate War* (Pantheon, 1974), *Monster* (HarperCollins, 1999), and *Looking for Alaska* (Dutton, 2005)—and demanded that we permanently remove them from our collection. She told the principal that the books were cited on an online list of banned books, and now he wants me to use the list to weed our collection. What should I do? *November 2009*

The principal isn't asking you to "weed" the collection. He's asking you to practice censorship. Do you have a materials selection and reconsideration policy? Without such a policy, a librarian is vulnerable to anyone who demands that materials be removed from the library.

If you have a policy, remind the principal that the parent needs to file a complaint and go through the formal reconsideration process. Most people don't want to go through a formal process. They prefer to make noise and bring school administrators to their knees. If you don't have a policy, this incident should serve as a wake-up call for you to develop one. Make sure your school board reviews it every few years. That way anyone who issues a challenge can't say your policy is out-of-date. Also, the next time you notice parents searching your shelves, ask if you can help them find what they're looking for. Then suggest that they read each title and come back and discuss them with you. A good conversation will almost always result in a positive outcome.

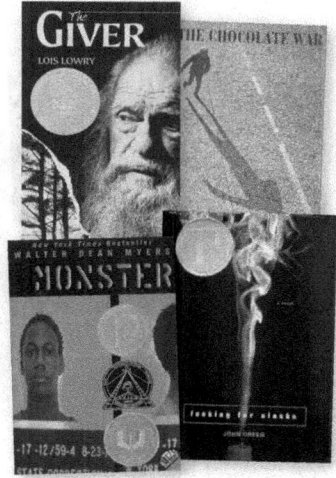

෩ ◎ ෬

There's a link on our public library's young adult page to a site that supports gay teens. Although a group of citizens (mostly out-of-towners) complained about the link, the library director has refused to take it down. The complaint was referred to the library's board, of which I'm the president. Since then, encouraged by local Christian radio and TV stations, the group has expanded its complaint to include books that it considers "pornographic," such as *The Perks of Being a Wallflower* (MTV, 1999), *Geography Club* (Harper Tempest, 2003), *Deal with It! A Whole New Approach to Your Body, Brain, and Life as a Gurl* (Pocket Books, 1999), and *It's Perfectly Normal: A Book About Changing Bodies, Growing Up, Sex, and Sexual Health* (4th Edition, Candlewick, 2014).

Since the group's complaint has substantially changed, the city attorney dismissed it. As a result, the group became outraged and launched a campaign against the library, its staff, and the library board, which has led to some of our members not being reappointed. The group has also inundated the city council with email messages and phone calls, and the controversy has become the focus of numerous sermons and letters to the editor of a local newspaper. At the moment, our public library has a terrible public relations problem. How do we combat censorship when there's no procedure for us to follow? *November 2009*

This is clearly the work of an organized group. Its tactics are very similar to groups

like PABBIS, or Parents Against Bad Books in Schools. They throw around terms like "pornography," and they advance their agendas by intimidation. This method of operation usually works with politicians like city council members who appoint the library board. The troubling part is that your city council has bowed to pressure from "outsiders." There is one part of your question that puzzles me. You indicate that you don't have a procedure to follow in censorship cases, yet the city attorney has dismissed the original complaint because it had substantially changed. That means there's some type of procedure—or perhaps he was just taking a legal stand. Follow his lead, and take time to address your library's policy and procedures. As president of the library board, you can make library policy an agenda item. Suggest to the board that it review policies from other public libraries that have similar demographics (you can often find a library's policy posted on its website). Caution the board that a policy should reflect the needs of the entire community, not just a select few. And reach out to the city attorney for help. He sounds like the library's new "best friend."

Finally, consider sponsoring a series of panel discussions about the issue and include young adults on the panels. They're the patrons who have suffered most from this incident. I've found that the voices of informed children and young adults can usually win over uninformed adults. I bet that these programs will have a positive impact on your library's image and make a significant difference from a public relations perspective.

ఴ ◎ ଓ

**A principal in our district has demanded that the librarian cut all magazine subscriptions. He insists that his request is budget related, but I've heard that some parents complained about the content in magazines such as *National Geographic* and *Seventeen*. Can we do anything to protect librarians from such requests?** *September 2009*

It sounds like this principal is using the economy as an excuse to commit an act of censorship. There will always be individual articles and ads that are troublesome to some readers, but patrons have the option of not reading that content. I might believe the principal's rationale if he had simply told the librarian to cut the budget and let her decide what to cut. The fact that he targeted magazines is very suspicious. Many school districts have districtwide library coordinators who deal with those kinds of problems. If you don't have one, find out who deals with library-related issues, and ask that person to convene a districtwide meeting of librarians to talk about this specific case. Also, check your district's materials selection policy. If there isn't a policy that deals with magazine subscriptions, now is the time to lobby for such a policy. Without one, librarians are vulnerable.

ཨ ◎ ཙ

**I recently read a discussion on LM_NET about *in loco parentis*, Latin for "in the place of a parent." There seems to be some confusion. One subscriber said that educators act *in loco parentis*, but I learned in library school that we don't have that sort of status. What's correct?**
*March 2009*

It varies from state to state. For example, the state of Washington has no in loco parentis statute. On the other hand, some states grant schools limited in loco parentis, which usually means "physical care and control." *In loco parentis* puts a lot of responsibility on a school's staff. It's a road I don't think anyone wants to go down if it's not required. For example, full *in loco parentis* status might require a library media specialist to keep a book about Islam out of the hands of a child whose parents are fundamentalist Christians and don't want him to read about any religion other than their own. Personally, I wouldn't want that kind of responsibility.

The in loco parentis argument is often used to justify a library professional's decision to avoid purchasing certain materials. Check your state law.

ཨ ◎ ཙ

I'm getting directives from teachers about which books certain kids can and can't check out. For instance, one parent told a teacher she doesn't want her son to be able to check out the "Captain Underpants" (Scholastic) series books from the library. I agreed to honor the re-

**quest, but now I feel like I've done something horribly wrong. What should I do?** *March 2009*
Your question is closely related to the issue of in loco parentis. The teacher shouldn't have made such a promise to the parent, and you shouldn't have agreed to honor the request. If the parent has a problem with her child reading "Captain Underpants" titles, then she needs to talk to her child about it. A library media specialist serves too many children to have the burden of this type of request. It's also a matter of professional ethics. Our role is to encourage, not discourage, reading.

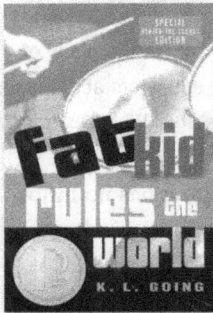

ဆ ◎ ಐ

My eighth graders love books like K. L. Going's *Fat Kid Rules the World* (Putnam, 2003). Although the novel's language is sometimes explicit, it seems to always fit the story. Since there's such a big difference between sixth graders' and eighth graders' maturity levels, how do I determine which books to buy for our middle school library? *January 2007*
*Fat Kid Rules the World* is an excellent novel for eighth graders, and a number of reviewers have recommended it for middle school collections. Explicit language shouldn't be a factor in determining whether to include a particular book in your collection—unless the story's potentially offensive language is gratuitous. Novels should be selected on the basis of literary merit and their overall appeal to the intended audience. Since you feel the language in *Fat Kid Rules the World* is appropriate and your students are crazy about the book, I'd recommend including it in your collection. I seriously doubt that many sixth graders will be drawn to Going's novel. My experience with middle schoolers is that most of them ultimately reject titles they're not ready for.

By the way, all too often teachers and librarians require kids to finish reading books they don't like. That's a powerful setup for reading failure, and may eventually lead to censorship problems. Allowing students to simply return books that don't interest them may eliminate most of your worries about the age appropriateness of certain titles.

ဆ ◎ ಐ

**If our reconsideration committee decides that a book is unsuitable for our collection, should the title be removed from every library in the district?** *January 2007*

Not necessarily. A reconsideration committee may decide that a book is unsuitable for an elementary school library, but appropriate for a middle or high school library. For example, Phyllis Reynolds Naylor's "Alice" series has been challenged in school districts nationwide. Some committees have said that *The Agony of Alice* (Atheneum, 1985), the series' first book, is fine for elementary school libraries, but subsequent books in the series (like *Achingly Alice*, *Alice Alone*, *Simply Alice*, and *Including Alice*), which follow the protagonist when she's a lot older, are more appropriate for middle school libraries. Luckily for readers, and for libraries, those reconsideration committees didn't ban the entire series—they offered a compromise. So everyone is a winner. By the way, Naylor has also written prequels that feature Alice as a young girl.

☙ ◎ ❧

**My district insists that a clergy member sit on our materials review committee. It just so happens that this particular member almost always votes against retaining challenged materials. Is it important to have religious representation?** *May 2007*

It's up to the school board to decide the makeup of the materials review committee. The religious community is so strong in some districts that it's wise to include them. Don't assume that every clergyperson will always vote against materials that have been challenged. Most will read or view the materials like any other committee member and offer an intelligent and thought provoking perspective. Their point of view may or may not be shared by other committee members, but it's important to include their opinion. The school board's policy should specify the length of service for committee members and set a rotating schedule. That way, there will always be an experienced person on your committee. The clergy position should rotate among the various religious faiths in the community. It's also a good idea to add a high school or middle school representative to your committee. Student voices are important, too.

☙ ◎ ❧

**Our district requires each of its schools to have a materials review committee, consisting of a principal or assistant principal, teachers, and parents. If somebody challenges a title and**

**disagrees with the school committee's decision, they're free to appeal the decision to a district-level committee. What are the advantages and disadvantages of our policy?** *May 2007*

Since you've asked, I assume that you feel your policy needs to be revised. Policies should be evaluated regularly and changed if they're not working well. There's no one policy that fits every district's needs. Remember, the most important element of a good materials review policy is that all parties have a say.

The benefits of having a school-level policy include the following:

- A potentially volatile situation may be contained by reasoning with the challenger.
- The challenge isn't a direct threat to the district's other schools.
- The complainant may be required to read or view the entire work before appealing the committee's decision.
- The challenger may be satisfied with an alternative materials choice, especially if they have felt empowered by the local school.

On the other hand, the problems or liabilities of your policy are:

- It's unlikely that a district-level appeal will be made if the challenged materials are removed.
- Faculty committee members may fear retaliation from the administration if a decision proves unpopular.
- It's difficult to elicit unbiased views when the committee members are coworkers or parents of students.
- A controversial decision could split the school community and damage relationships among teachers and parents.

Even if a district doesn't have a materials review committee at the school level, most districts require schools to get involved in the first step of a challenge. For example, if somebody challenges a title, they should be encouraged to talk to a teacher or librarian before appealing to the administration. If the issue still can't be resolved, then a formal challenge must be made in writing.

80 ◎  08

**I'm an elementary school media specialist in a very conservative community, and I'd like to add Louis Sachar's *Small Steps* (Delacorte, 2006) to my library collection. But I'm wor-**

ried that the book may be challenged because it contains the word "crap." What should I do? *November 2006*

There's always a chance that someone will challenge our book selection choices. But words that a potential censor might find offensive shouldn't affect our purchasing decisions, as long as the language isn't gratuitous. A librarian should make an objective decision about a book's appeal to her students. *Small Steps* is recommended for grades five to eight, which means the book is deemed appropriate for those in upper elementary grades. Fans of *Holes* by the same author will want to read this companion novel about Armpit's fate as he sets out to overcome past demons. Young readers shouldn't be denied access to this novel because of a potentially offensive word. However, as a precautionary measure, find out what your school or district's selection policy says about books with offensive language. You likely won't need it, but make sure there's a materials reconsideration procedure should a challenge occur.

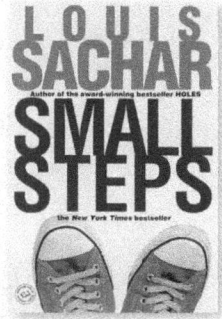

# 2

# *Censorship via Physical Access, Defacing Books, and More*

### Restricted shelves in K12 and
### public library settings, YA sections, and more

Access to a book can be limited in a number of ways even after it has been added to the collection. Such restrictions should be avoided when introduced as an alternative and they should be reversed when discovered. In several entries here, Scales re-asserts a child's right to open access to the materials in the collection. This means having coherent, consistent, transparent policies through the collection development process. This means having the books vailable and on the shelves. More overt restrictions like requiring parental permission to look at a book or holding books in the director's office are not acceptable practice. Several librarians querying Scales had to contend with requests to deface books by blacking out specific words or passages. One very interesting theme that emerges in this chapter is the wisdom of the reader: children, Scales, reminds us will turn away books that they are not ready for out of sheer boredom. Efforts are better utilized in engaging kids in materials than looking for things to keep away from them.—*R. T. M.*

**I'm a teen librarian in a small public library. We have had so many challenges to YA literature that the library director has suggested that we merge the teen and adult collection. She thinks this may eliminate some of the issues.** *September 2014*

A library that has a sudden increase in the number of challenges is likely the target of an organized group. It's frustrating to deal with such groups because they mobilize via the Internet and are relentless. I'm sure you must have a selection policy that includes a reconsideration process. This should be followed to a tee. Require that those bringing the challenges complete the form in its entirety. My bet is that these people haven't read the books. They have a right to challenge, but they don't have a right to control the way the library serves its patrons.

I sense that the library director is simply tired of constantly dealing with challenges, but to merge the collections would not solve the problem. What would happen to the teen program if this were done? Would teens even want to come to the library if identifying interesting books is so difficult? Teens need to be embraced, not dismissed.

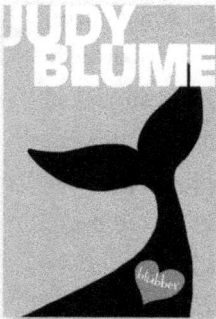

෨ ◎ ଔ

**Judy Blume's *Blubber* (Bradbury, 1974) was recently challenged at my elementary school because of "profanity and the way the kids treat one another." The Materials Review Committee recommended that the book be retained, but the superintendent ordered me to place the novel on a "restricted" shelf and limit access to fifth graders. This sets a precedent that labeling and restricting books are okay, but I don't know how to argue my case to remove the restriction.** *June 2014*

I want to outline a court case involving "restricted" shelves and minor's rights. In 2002, the school board in Cedarville, Arkansas, ordered that all "Harry Potter" books (Scholastic) be removed from the open shelves and held in the office of the librarians, and circulated only to the students with parental permission. Parents of a fourth grader sued the school district, because they felt their child's First Amendment rights had been violated and that having to present permission "stigmatized" their child as "evil" in the eyes of other students and their parents. The district court agreed. The court also stated, "There was no evidence to support the school district's claim that the books would promote disobedience, disrespect for authority, or disruption in school."

While the case in your school is different from the Arkansas case, it's unlikely that the courts would uphold the action taken by your superintendent, because library materials may not be removed due to "personal biases and opinions" of a librarian, teacher, or administrator. The case in Cedarville clearly stated "restriction" is the same as "removing" a book. My bet is that your superintendent doesn't have a clue about the potential "uproar" he could cause by denying open access to the book.

This statement from ALA may give you language to use when making your case: Access to Library Resources and Services for Minors - An Interpretation of the Library Bill of Rights (see addendum, p. 134).

∞ ◎ ∞

A third-grade teacher in my school has Nancy Farmer's *The House of the Scorpion* (Atheneum, 2002) in her classroom library. She told her students that they could read the book if they got written permission from their parents. Parents are asking my opinion. I didn't purchase the book for the elementary library, but I understand that the book is a big hit in the neighboring middle school. What should I say to parents without making this teacher look bad? *November 2013*

*The House of the Scorpion* is an excellent novel, but I doubt that many third graders will be drawn to it. Tell the parents that the book is a better choice for middle school students because of its complex themes and conflict. I recommend that you explain to the teacher that it isn't a good idea to have any book in the classroom that requires parental permission. Such a practice sends a red flag that can cause nothing but trouble from parents and make students think that the novel deals with "forbidden" subject matter. This isn't a good message for readers of any age. Also, tell the teacher that you didn't choose the novel for your library because reviewers recommend it for older readers, and offer to help her select books for her classroom library.

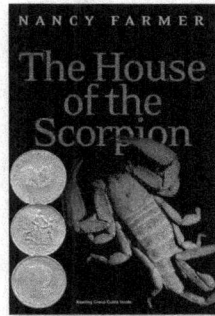

∞ ◎ ∞

We've always kept Robie Harris's books in our children's room. But after a mother complained about them, our public library director asked us to put the titles in our teen collection. Although I was reluctant to move them, I felt I had to comply. Is this a form of censorship? *November 2011*

Yes. Harris's books are written for children and families and should be available in your children's collection. I've heard the argument from public library directors, and some children's librarians, that since kids are allowed to have unrestricted access to the entire collection, it doesn't matter where the books are kept. But if the books are intended for children, they should be available where kids are most likely to find them—and that's in the children's room.

Moving books is a coward's way out and, in the end, doesn't solve the problem. What will you do when a parent complains about *My Mom's Having a Baby!* (Albert Whitman, 2005) or *Where Willy Went* (Knopf, 2005)? These are clearly picture books with no teen appeal.

ဢ ◎ ଔ

**I purchased a book on war weapons based on our world history teachers' recommendations and on reviews I'd read. But when the book arrived, I found it very disturbing—it was just too graphic. I'm not comfortable adding the book to our collection, but our teachers want their students to have access to it. Should I put it in our professional collection for teachers to use? Or should I return the book?** *August 2010*

You purchased the book based on teacher recommendations and book reviews. That means that you performed your role as a librarian. Another part of that role is to put the book in your collection so that students can use it. There are probably a number of books in your collection that you may personally dislike or find difficult to defend. But a school librarian must remain objective and serve the needs of students and faculty. Putting the book in the professional collection is the same as placing it on a restricted shelf.

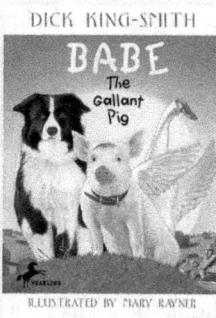

ဢ ◎ ଔ

DICK KING-SMITH

BABE
The
Gallant
Pig

ILLUSTRATED BY MARY RAYNER

**One of our teachers is upset because I recommended that her students read *Dick King-Smith's Babe: The Gallant Pig* (Crown, 1985), which refers to a female dog as a "bitch." The teacher would like to use Phyllis Reynolds Naylor's Newbery Award winning book *Shiloh* (Atheneum, 1991) with her class, but she's reluctant to do that because it contains the word "dammit." The teacher's solution? She wants me to delete the word. I told her I wouldn't, but she won't listen to reason. What should I do?** *May 2010*

Check your state laws. In some states, it's a misdemeanor to deface a book. If your state has such a law, post it in the library. Legal or not, there's an ethical issue here. Ask the teacher what she would do if a student crossed out a word from a textbook. I bet she'd probably insist that the student pay for the book. Students need to know that "bitch" is a female dog, and they need to understand why a character like Judd Travers, in *Shiloh*, would scream "dammit" at his dogs. Perhaps you should offer to lead that part of the book discussion with her students.

ಬ © ಛ

**Our school library serves students in grades 7–12, but some of our books are too mature for seventh and eighth graders. I want to preserve students' freedom to read, but I worry that a book like Toni Morrison's *Beloved* (Knopf, 1987) might get into younger students' hands. Would it be OK if I set up a section of the library that's strictly for high school students?** *January 2009*

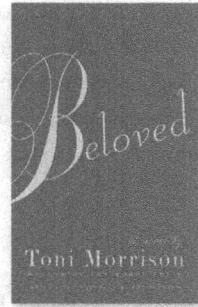

That's not a good idea. I grew up in a school that served students in grades one to eight, and the library was a combination school/town library. I went there every afternoon after school and often during the summer, and I checked out whatever I wanted to read. I don't remember a section for "adults only" or one labeled "for mature readers." It just wasn't an issue. Over my long career, I've learned that children will put down books they aren't ready for. The great majority of seventh and eighth graders won't be interested in reading *Beloved*. But some kids will, and they should be allowed to read it. A restricted area of the library isn't the answer. Students almost always gravitate to the "forbidden." The best thing to do is to encourage students to quit reading books that don't interest them. Most of your younger students won't make it past the first chapter of *Beloved*. They'll be more intrigued by your young adult titles. Think about this: How do you judge the maturity level of a book? There are many YA novels that deal with subjects and themes as challenging as those in Morrison's works.

ಬ © ಛ

**I'm about to replace an elementary school librarian who has had the job for 35 years. When I visited the school, I noticed that the picture books and fiction were shelved on the bottom three shelves, and nonfiction was shelved on the top shelves. When I inquired about this ar-**

rangement, the librarian told me that only fourth and fifth graders were allowed to check out nonfiction; so she kept those titles out of the reach of younger children. Is that censorship? I intend to change this practice, but I'm afraid I'll meet with opposition from the faculty. By the way, this is my first library position. *September 2009*

Yes, such denial of access is an act of censorship. There are so many good works of nonfiction for younger readers that I cringe at the thought that anyone would deny children the opportunity to read them. I hope that you change this practice your first day on the job. I seriously doubt that you'll meet with any opposition. I bet the faculty is ready for such a change. I suggest having a library open house for faculty and staff. Display outstanding works of nonfiction, and invite faculty to brainstorm ways that they might use nonfiction in their classrooms. Let them know that children have a genuine interest in informational books, and that nonfiction is so celebrated that the Association of Library Service to Children awards the Sibert Medal annually to an outstanding work of nonfiction for children. Good Luck.

ɝ ◎ ɞ

*Sports Illustrated* is popular with our middle schoolers, but some of its content is too mature for them. (The annual swimsuit issue usually ends up in our principal's office.) Should I purchase a subscription or are we better off without it? *March 2007*

Middle school students are interested in sports, and they're too old to read *Sports Illustrated Kids*. When I worked at a middle school, I subscribed to *Sports Illustrated* and placed the swimsuit issue on our shelves. Not surprisingly, some of its pages always disappeared. But I'm still glad that issue was available to our students, because it showed that we respected them. Remember, just because you purchase library books and magazines doesn't mean you're personally endorsing every page. I'd recommend that you ask your principal to leave the swimsuit edition in the library. Also, how do you handle *National Geographic, Ebony, Teen People*, and *Seventeen*? Those magazines, among many others, have editorial content and ads that some people may find objectionable. But teens are interested in those publications and should have access to them.

ɝ ◎ ɞ

Our school purchased 900 copies of Sean Covey's *The Seven Habits of Highly Effective Teens* (Simon & Schuster, Fireside, 1998) for our students, but the principal and district administrators were offended by one of its phrases: "You're not ready to have sex if...." So they've had the phrase covered with a sticker that says, "Fifty reasons not to have sex." Is that legal? By the way, we offer the book in our library collection—without the sticker. *May 2007* Some states have a law that prohibits anyone from defacing a work of literature or art. My advice is to find out if your state has such a law, and if it does, make sure your administrators are aware of it. Ask whoever selected the title to meet with your administrators and explain how the selection process works and how the book will be used. My guess is that your administrators haven't read the entire book—they're only reacting to what they see as a potential challenge from parents. Good for you for putting an "uncensored" copy of the book in the library. The actions of the administrators have shown great disrespect to your students, and they've sent a message that censorship is OK. I can assure you that students will try to peel off the stickers. Once they discover that you have the book in its original form, they'll flock to the library to read it.

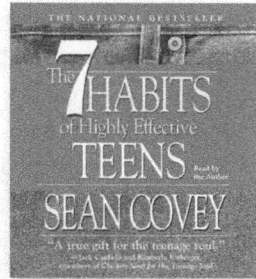

෨ ◎ ෬

**A very active member of the PTA has asked that I place the very popular Philip Pullman books on a restricted shelf in my middle school library and require parental consent to read them—all because they deal with evil forces. What should I say?** *November 2006*
The answer is simple: No! And there's legal precedent to back you up. In 2002, the board of the Cedarville School District in Arkansas voted 3-2 in favor of students needing parental permission to borrow Harry Potter books. The parents of an avid Potter fan took the school board to court because they felt it was a violation of their daughter's constitutional rights. U.S. District Judge Jimm Larry Hendren ruled, "Regardless of the personal distaste with which these individuals regard 'witchcraft,' it is not properly within their power and authority as members of the defendant's school board to prevent the students at Cedarville from reading about it." Cedarville students now have free access to Harry Potter and any number of fantasy titles. Parents can prevent their children from reading certain novels, or even entire genres, but librarians don't exist to help parents police their children.

Refer to the American Library Association's Library Bill of Rights for more information about supporting an open access policy. Restricted Access to Library Materials: An Interpretation of the Library Bill of Rights (adopted by ALA's Council

February 2, 1973, and most recently amended in July 2014) states, "All proposals for restricted access should be carefully scrutinized to ensure that the purpose is not to suppress a viewpoint or to place a barrier between users and content. Libraries must maintain policies and procedures that serve the diverse needs of their users and protect the First Amendment right to receive information."

# 3

# *Labeling*

## Never a good idea

"My advice is to neither label nor limit," writes Scales in response to a librarian in a quandry about how to best guide the young readers she serves. Labels, often intended to either promote titles to a special segment of readers, have the unfortunate ricochet effect of too tightly defining who is the "right" reader for a book or collection. This problem applies to reading levels as well, which are not oriented to a particular child's interests or ability and, as Scales describes, can actually backfire by pointing children to a range of books they are not ready for and limiting their access to books that would better engage them. Labels are never, according to Scales, an effective entree to the library's collection. Most likely an adult will need to be there to help from time to time—and that's a good thing, too.—*R. T. M.*

**A local women's organization has complained that our public library doesn't have enough books that present a positive image of women and girls. I pointed out a number of titles, but they want them labeled with a girl silhouette so that girls may spot them quickly. This isn't something that the library wants to do, but this organization is taking the issue to the library board.** *September 2014*

Hopefully the library board will leave this decision to the professional staff. Does the library have a policy on labeling? New issues related to labeling are cropping up in public and school libraries. The American Library Association recently updated its statement on labeling and made it available on the Office for Intellectual Freedom website (see link in the addendum, p.135). It can serve as a guide for libraries as they update their own policies.

I'm sure the women's organization has good intentions, but labeling books is a slippery slope. Male readers may not give books like Christopher Paul Curtis's *The Mighty Miss Malone* (Random, 2012), Kate DiCamillo's *Because of Winn-Dixie* (Candlewick, 2000), or Jacqueline Kelly's *The Evolution of Calpurnia Tate* (Holt, 2009) a chance if they are labeled with a girl symbol. Suggest that the library provide a bibliography of books with strong female characters for the organization to distribute to members or on their website if they have one. Let them know that the library will work with them and provide a display for Women's History Week in March. Suggest that the organization develop a brochure that lists such titles and place it in bookstores in town.

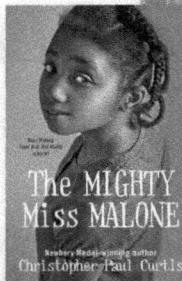

ഇ ◎ ര

**I'm a director of a small public library. The children's librarian asked me if it's okay to label books by Lexile Reading Levels. I have an ethical problem with this, but parents are requesting it, which presents a dilemma.** *February 2014*

You are absolutely right that such labeling is an ethical issue. I understand the dilemma, but labeling reading materials based on reading levels sends the wrong message to readers and their parents. The Lexile Framework for Reading website claims to match readers with texts, but the system looks at the readability of a text and not the maturity level. This type of labeling has actually created censorship problems because eight-year-olds reading on an eighth-grade level are led to books for which they aren't yet emotionally ready. It's equally important to consider children with deficient reading skills. They should be allowed to read what interests them, even if the material is a little difficult. Offer the good reader guidance that public libraries have long been noted for.

℘ ◎ ℅

**I'm a library school student, and I just completed an internship at an elementary school. When I first got there, I was excited to learn that the school didn't use Accelerated Reader, because I don't think that students should be asked to take a test on every book they read. Then I discovered that the teachers limited their students to reading books that were on their reading level. I was assigned to label all of the library's books according to the Fountas & Pinnell assessment system. I'm uncomfortable with labeling, but I had to do it to get credit for my internship. What should I do in the future if I'm asked to do something that goes against my educational philosophy?** *May 2010*

I'm glad that you were uncomfortable with this assignment. It shows that you really care about children's enjoyment of reading. I recommend that you discuss your philosophy at your job interviews. If you're lucky, you may find an enlightened principal who'll support you in creating a library where children can discover the joy of reading. After you've started your new job, it's possible that you may be able to convince an administrator to phase out leveling. Push your point by giving a child a book that's far above her predetermined reading level—a title you know she'll enjoy. When she's finished reading it, invite the principal to listen to her talk about the book. After the discussion, reveal the book's reading level to your principal. Case closed.

℘ ◎ ℅

**For years I've worked at a school that serves seventh and eighth graders. But recently, we've also added sixth grade. For the first time in my career, I feel as though I'm guilty of self-censoring. Some of the books that were fine for eighth graders, like John Marsden's *Letters from the Inside* (Houghton Mifflin, 1994), don't seem age-appropriate for sixth graders. What should I do? Should I label the more mature titles so our younger students won't be surprised by the content? Or should I limit the sixth graders to one section of the library?** *May 2010*

My advice is to neither label nor limit. If you label the books for "Mature Readers,"

the entire student body will soon be combing your shelves, trying to pick out the "mature" parts of those titles. Taking content out of context can send a message that ultimately plays into the hands of censors. And please, don't relegate sixth graders to one small area of the library. Give them room to explore and grow. Yes, there are some very mature sixth graders in your school, but there are also some immature eighth graders. You need to meet all of their needs. Some publishers include a recommended age range on their book covers (for example, for ages 14 and up). Although librarians aren't expected to remove that information, they shouldn't use it to limit their patrons' access to those titles.

Talk with your students about what they're reading, lead them to books you think they'll enjoy, and give them permission to reject titles they don't like. Most of all, teach them to look at an entire book before judging its individual parts. If a book has tough characters, talk to students about those characters. If a book includes profanity, talk about why the characters may use it. By asking young readers the right questions, you're teaching them how to analyze a book—and you're modeling the principles of intellectual freedom. The next time students happen upon a book they feel is too mature, they'll either reject it, or read it and see it differently.

ℰ ◎ ℬ

**I read that Philip Pullman and many other children's book creators have taken a strong stance against publishers putting recommended reading ages on book covers. I depend on that information when I'm selecting titles for our library. Why are so many writers and illustrators against it?** *September 2008*

Librarians and parents have long depended on publishers' age-guidance recommendations. It's helpful information, as long as it isn't misused. Pullman and more than 700 children's book authors and illustrators have signed a statement against this type of guidance, feeling that it stigmatizes young readers. I have no doubt that their radical position grew out of a frustration with the growing number of children's titles that have reading-level labels. But there's a huge difference between the two types of labels. Reading level stigmatizes, while age guidance proposes a targeted audience. Anytime labels are used to restrict readers, censorship has occurred. It's helpful to remember that children's book authors and illustrators care deeply about their creations, and most feel that their books have no age limitations. When the film of Pullman's *The Golden Compass* was released last year, it attracted scores of censors. Perhaps that's what sparked his ardent efforts to change the way the public views books, especially those for young readers. (To find out more about Pullman's "No to Age Banding" crusade, visit www. notoagebanding.org.)

Reviews of children's books almost always include age guidance, such as for ages 6–8, 9–12, 12 up, or 14 up. It's important that librarians use these recommendations judicially. After all, there are many eight-year-olds who are ready to read books that are published for 10- and 12-year-olds. One of the roles of a librarian is to offer youngsters a wide range of reading materials—without placing any restrictions on them.

Keep in mind that there are many kids' books that appeal to adults, too, including J. R. R. Tolkien's *The Hobbit* (Houghton Mifflin, 1966); Lois Lowry's *The Giver* (Houghton Mifflin, 1993); C. S. Lewis's *The Lion, the Witch, and the Wardrobe* (HarperCollins, 1950); and Pullman's "His Dark Materials" trilogy (Knopf). Novels with that kind of crossover appeal should be included in a library's adult collection as well as in its children's collection. That practice makes a statement similar to what Pullman is advocating: books have no age restrictions; they're written for whoever wants to read them.

৪০ ◎ ଷ

**A parent of one of our first graders filed a formal complaint against Alvin Schwartz's *Scary Stories to Tell in the Dark* (Lippincott, 1981), claiming the book had frightened her child and it shouldn't be read by elementary school students. Our materials review committee voted to retain the title, but recommended that a label be placed on it that says "Fourth Grade & Up." The school board honored the recommendation. What should I do if a younger student wants to read it?** *March 2007*

A library should be open and not restrictive in its practices. It's too bad that the materials review committee issued such a request. Since the board supported the recommendation, you'll have to put a label on the book. But that doesn't mean you have to restrict access to it.

A 2003 federal court ruling states that books may not be placed on a restricted shelf because of their content. The case involved an elementary school in Cedarville, AR, that restricted access to its Harry Potter books because some parents thought they were "evil." The ruling supports your right to make *Scary Stories* available to all readers.

Schwartz's book is based on folklore, and many youngsters have read it without experiencing an ounce of fear. I don't think that even the best first- and second-grade readers can read it independently. It's likely that they'll need adult assistance. Isn't that what we want, anyway? Engaged parents!

# 4

# *Confronting Rating Systems*

## Media, Accelerated Reader, and more

There's no doubt that libraries, and especially school libraries, are there and ready to help support the curriculum being deployed, but, as Scales describes in several entries here, their mandate is to also support developing readers. These dual mandates can put libraries at odds with strategies that tend to keep kids too focused on the task of learning and not focused enough on the value of reading for fun. While working with reading levels is a reality, keeping the library a vibrant space for further exploration is imperative. Rating strategies too often act as barriers, keeping kids from discovering new things based on their own interest instead of their reading level. This approach extends to transforming the impulse to restrict access into a conversation that can be its own teaching moment about the complexity and thematics of a story or film. Because reading levels are so tightly tied to curricular goals, notes Scales, it's important to demonstrate the power of free reading to administrators and thereby foster a supportive environment for the entire library and reading program.—*R. T. M.*

**My school uses a computerized reading program that assigns reading levels to students. I've been asked to label our library books and restrict students to their appropriate reading levels. Is that acceptable?** *September 2006*

The American Library Association discourages placing prejudicial labels on library materials. Some school librarians may argue that labeling and shelving books by grade level makes it easier for children to find titles that correspond to their reading levels. But that scenario becomes censorship when students are only allowed to take out materials that match their reading levels. Although some parents and teachers think that labeling books by grade level is helpful in guiding young readers, libraries should never use labels that promote restrictive or prejudicial practices. By the way, most computerized reading programs provide the grade levels of books on their Web sites for those seeking such information.

&#128;&#9678;&#8506;

**The district just told us that we can't use any upper-level Accelerated Reader books in our elementary school reading program because the topics may be too mature for our students. We think they're censoring the program and our students will suffer.** *March 2012*

I'd say the students are the winners. Maybe they can finally read books that interest them without being tested on everything they read. This doesn't mean that you can't have these books in the library. The students will reject whichever ones they can't handle.

&#128;&#9678;&#8506;

**Our public library serves several elementary schools that use Accelerated Reader (AR). Some of the parents and board members are asking me to put AR reading level stickers on books in our children's collection. I don't like this type of labeling, but I'm getting pressured. What should I do?** *March 2012*

Check to see if your library has a policy that prohibits that type of labeling. If it does, then you need only point to the policy. Talk with those who want the books labeled and explain that reading levels are determined "scientifically" and that you prefer to encourage children to read for enjoyment and for deeper meanings than AR emphasizes. You might also want to remind them that most schools that use AR have a link on their website to a list of AR books that are arranged by reading levels, and it's easy for parents and students to access that information. Don't waste your money on labels. That way, you'll have more to spend on new library books.

**As a boy approached our circulation desk with a copy of Jerry Spinel-li's *Wringer* (HarperCollins, 1997), his mother grabbed it and said, "I just checked reviews of that book on my iPhone, and I think there's sexual content and violence." They got into a tug-of-war, and I didn't know what to do.** *September 2011*

It's tough to come between a parent and a child, but I'd ask to speak with the parent privately. I'd tell her about the book and let her know that rating systems are subjective and they may only express one reviewer's opinion. Explain how *Wringer*'s words and scenes are taken out of context, and that rating systems actually devalue children's literature, because they shift the focus away from the work's true meaning. Suggest that the mother and son both read *Wringer* and talk about it afterward. My bet is that she'll be very surprised by her child's insights. If she refuses to do that, there isn't much you can do other than to direct the student to another book.

If we don't make reader guidance one of our top priorities, rating systems can potentially overshadow the good work we librarians do. It's essential that your staff members receive proper training in reader guidance techniques and that they know they're expected to read as many new acquisitions as possible. At your next staff meeting, take a look at some of the rating systems and discuss why these systems have become a tool for censors. All of us need to understand what we're up against.

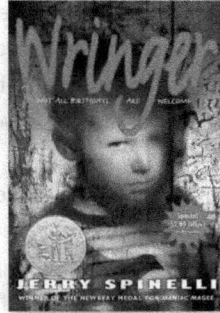

ഇ ◎ ൧

**When a friend found out that the school library had restricted her second-grade son to books that corresponded to his reading level, she requested that he be given access to the entire collection. The librarian and principal eventually agreed that he could have full use of the library after school, but they won't allow other students to have similar access. My friend wonders if that's censorship.** *November 2011*

Yes, it's censorship. The most frightening part is the principal's and librarian's attitudes. Children should be allowed to explore whatever interests them regardless of a book's reading level. School librarians feel they have to support the reading curriculum, but that doesn't mean they need to restrict students' access to the library's collection. For example, young children with a passion for dinosaurs can handle informational books about them that are written at a high reading level because they're interested in the subject. Encourage your friend to rally other parents around this issue—it might be the only way to change the school library's restrictive policy.

I inherited a library collection that troubles me. Eighty percent of our fiction and 20 percent of our nonfiction have reading level labels and Accelerated Reader's (AR) big red dots on their spines. When students browse the books, they search by labels rather than by title or author. Also, their teachers have instructed them to check out two AR books and one "fun" book. Is our goal to support the curriculum, even if it means allowing a commercial reading program to dictate how our collection is arranged? Or is our goal to provide an open library where students are encouraged to browse materials based on their interests? There seems to be a conflict between these goals. Also, have you heard of any librarians who have removed the labels and rearranged their collections according to author or Dewey number? *January 2010*

The mission of the school library is to support the curriculum and to provide materials and services that satisfy the interests and needs of all children. There shouldn't be a conflict between these two goals. The most troubling part of your situation is that teachers don't equate reading with fun. Though I don't like anything about AR, I do know that there are AR books that might be fun to read. But the fun is squelched when students have to take a test on every title they read. A library doesn't have to succumb to labeling just because the school district uses AR. I suggest you remove all of the labels. Bookmark AR's Web site on your library computers and show students and teachers how to use the site to identify books that are appropriate for the child's reading level. Then ask students to locate books by author or Dewey classification. I also suggest that you move forward with library programming that promotes reading for fun. I don't know of a library that has reversed the practice of labeling books by AR reading levels. I do know that there are many frustrated librarians who dream of the day when students will once again come to the library in search of books that have no labels.

ဆ ◎ ଔ

In (an earlier) column I asked readers to write me if they had reversed their school's practice of putting Accelerated Reader (AR) labels on library books. I was surprised by how many librarians responded. Here's a sampling of some of the messages I received. Please keep sending me your success stories; they may appear in future columns. *March 2010*

When I moved from an elementary school that labeled its library books to a new school, one of the first things I did was to meet with our new principal. I knew that many of the teachers from my former school would be moving along with me and many of them liked AR labels on our library books. I explained that as a result of labeling, our students had no idea how to choose books that really interested them and if the practice continued, they'd never be prepared to use a regular library. Our principal said that he appreciated my passion for wanting our students to learn the right way to use a library and to develop a love of reading. So he very strongly supported my decision to stop labeling books. When the school opened, the decision was met with some resistance from teachers and parents, but having the support of the administration made all the difference. I'll never forget my students' reaction when they came into the library for the first time. I opened my arms, and told them they were free to choose whatever books they wanted to read, and the kids actually applauded! If you're still unsure about doing away with labels, I'd recommend reading Kelly Gallagher's *Readicide: How Schools Are Killing Reading and What You Should Do About It* (Stenhouse Publishers). —*Valerie Kinney, media coordinator, West View Elementary School, Johnston, NC*

When I arrived at our middle school as the new librarian, I quickly learned that AR was heavily emphasized in the fifth and sixth-grade curriculums. And I was dismayed when I discovered that many of the library books had AR labels on them. Our teachers use extrinsic rewards to encourage students to earn as many AR points as possible, so our students are very aware of the number of points each book is worth. Although it's hard for me to fight the reward system, I decided not to put AR labels on our new acquisitions. I haven't removed the labels from our old books, but as I weed our collection and add new titles, the labeled books are becoming less prominent. Not putting AR labels on new books hasn't been a popular decision with many of our teachers, and most of them still label their own classroom libraries. Although I can't put a stop to what our teachers are doing with AR, I can point out the intrinsic rewards of reading to students when I talk to them one-on-one, and I can do lots of readers' advisory with them, too. —*Rebecca Bock, teacher librarian, Winterset (IA) Elementary and Middle School*

**A school board in West Virginia wants to label high school books—similar to the way that movies are now rated. If they do that, I'm worried it will have a negative effect on students.**
*May 2008*

It sounds like you're referring to the case at Nitro High School in Charleston, WV, where two of Pat Conroy's books were banned. Apparently, the local school board thought that labeling books will help parents make better decisions for their kids. But that's opening a giant can of worms, and it raises some disturbing questions. For example, will a rating be determined, in part, by the number of four-letter words in the text? Will a book with a single sex scene be treated differently than one with three sex scenes? How will violence be defined? And what about thorny issues like abortion, euthanasia, and torture? Will contemporary fiction be scrutinized more closely than the classics or historical fiction? Will a story be allowed to include anti-American acts or anti-religious themes? And what about fantasy and science fiction? How will they be evaluated?

I can't imagine school board members will take the time to read every book in the English curriculum. So most likely, the job of rating books will fall upon the teachers. I worry that topnotch English teachers who are asked to "censor" books will lose their passion for teaching the great works of literature. If that happens, then their students would be the real losers. Placing ratings on books is also an insult to students' intelligence and could have a chilling effect on preparing them for college.

Talking about books—not banning them—is the best solution, and students should feel free to express their opinions. The only way a young person can develop an informed opinion is to read widely and deeply. The irony of the situation in West Virginia is that students are likely to read all of Conroy's works simply because they've been told not to read them.

Still, there's a ray of hope. Historically, school boards that have embraced "unreasonable" ways of dealing with objectionable materials have changed their minds once the brouhaha died down and they discovered their policies were too difficult to enforce.

ഇ ◎ ର

**I'm sick and tired of teachers coming into the library and telling students that they can't check out certain books because they're not the appropriate reading level. Isn't that censorship? By the way, my principal loves Accelerated Reader. How can I convince her that students should be free to make their own reading selections?** *January 2008*

This issue is a big problem in many of our nation's schools, and I get numerous emails about it. Here are some suggestions to help do away with restrictive labeling:

◎ Don't put a limit on the number of books that students can check out at any one time.

◎ A teacher may instruct her class to only take out books on their reading level, but you can get around that by encouraging kids to take out additional titles of their choice.

◎ Don't put reading level stickers on your books—it encourages labeling.

◎ Begin a student book club that meets before or after school, and be sure to introduce its members to all types of books.

◎ Find a teacher who's willing to "step out of the box" and suggest that the two of you conduct an experiment. Introduce students to books that interest them and that are supposedly too difficult for them. After the kids have read these titles, talk to them about the books, and invite your principal to the discussion. My bet is that your students will change your principal's mind about free reading.

∞ ◎ ೞ

**Our high school's English teachers have asked me to order a few different versions of the film** *Romeo and Juliet.* **Some of them are R-rated, and my colleagues plan to fast-forward through the nude scenes or cover the monitor with a towel. If I purchase the films, am I setting us up for a censorship challenge?** *March 2007*

Since *Romeo and Juliet* is taught in most high schools, it's reasonable for your colleagues to expect you to honor their requests. As for film ratings, when the Motion Picture Association of America (MPAA) assigns them, it doesn't take into account a movie's educational value. In fact, MPAA's ratings are simply private advisory codes and aren't legally binding. I'd advise teachers not to skip over the racy scenes. High school students are mature enough to handle them. Instead of thinking of ways to avoid those scenes, teachers should discuss them with their students before and after viewing the films.

Your school district may already have a selection policy. Some districts don't allow R-rated movies, and others frown on the use of full-length feature films because they take time away from traditional classroom instruction. If your school has a selection policy in place, share it with the faculty. If it doesn't, it's time to push for one.

# 5

# *Kids and Privacy*

## Reading choices, monitoring, and confidentiality

The benefits of a culture that supports and protects the private exploration of ideas extends to children, and YAs, as do legislated rights to kids' privacy in most states, notes Scales. This powerful theme recurs throughout this compilation but is detailed in this chapter via several examples from librarians striving to retain privacy even in simple ways for the kids using their libraries. Scales re-asserts an ethos that does not intrude in a person's use of the library, not by comparing one student to another nor by passing judgment on an an indidual child's choice. With the rise of digital applications that are designed to mine student activity to help track progress, the issue of privacy enters a new era to be grappled with with the same kid gloves. Librarians will need to be more vigilant than ever and rely on guidance from the American Library Association to approach the challenge ahead coherently.—*R. T. M.*

The central district administrators in my school district have developed an app for parents that includes all kinds of K–12 student data (grades, lunch balance, library records, etc.). I can see how this is a benefit to parents, but I feel that students' library records should remain private. Since students aren't given an opportunity to opt out, I'm afraid that this may have a chilling effect on student library use. Do parents have the right to obtain their children's library records? *June 2014*

Most states have privacy laws, and many do extend privacy rights to K–12 students. Not all, but a number of states actually protect children's library records from their parents. All librarians should check their state laws and post the pertinent law in the library so that students, teachers, administrators, and parents are informed. Protecting students' privacy is an ethical issue, even if there is no state law that grants them that right. Familiarize yourself with the valuable Privacy Toolkit, one that specifically pertains to schools and youth, on the ALA/OIF website.

ဆ ◎ ର

Our assistant principal found a library book on the cafeteria floor. He wanted me to tell him who had checked it out, so he could tell the student that he'd have to pay for any lost books. I responded by asking the administrator to put the book in our book drop. He was furious. *November 2012*

You did the right thing. This is a confidentiality issue, and I'd hope that the administration understands that. Kids drop as many books as Hansel and Gretel did bread crumbs. The important part is that the books usually find their way home.

ဆ ◎ ର

Our elementary school library's parent volunteers don't understand the importance of confidentiality. In fact, one of them even told her fifth-grade daughter that a particular classmate wasn't a good reader and still checked out Beverly Cleary books (William Morrow). Any advice? *September 2012*

Parent volunteers can be invaluable, especially when you're short-staffed, but it's important that they understand their role. At the beginning of the school year, offer a workshop for your volunteers. Tell them that library records are confidential, and you'd prefer to do all of the reader guidance yourself, since you understand students' reading preferences. Keep the problematic parent on your radar screen and give her a job that doesn't require interaction with students—there are always books to be shelved.

ಐ ◎ ಅ

**When our principal asked a seventh grader to tell him the name of the book he'd just checked out, the boy ran off without telling him. The principal asked me the book's title, but I refused to reveal it because that would've violated student privacy. What should I have done?** *March 2012*

You did exactly what you should have done. The fact that the student ran off should have been a clue that he didn't want to share his reading choice with the principal. The puzzling part of this scenario is that your principal asked you to reveal what the student had borrowed. If your state has a privacy law, post it in the library so that students, teachers, and administrators are aware of it. Even if your state doesn't have one, student circulation records should be kept confidential. That's the ethical thing to do.

ಐ ◎ ಅ

**Recently, two fathers came into our library with their young son and asked for some books about gay families. I was pointing out several possibilities when a woman tapped me on the shoulder and said, "I don't think you should be helping these men." I didn't know how to respond, and now I'm afraid she's going to cause trouble in our conservative community.** *September 2011*

You simply need to say, "Excuse me, they need my help." The public library serves everyone in the community, and that's all that needs to be said should the woman choose to turn serving gay families into an issue.

# 6

# *Confronting Censorship in Public Libraries*

### An inclusive mission, homeschooling, the importance of book reconsideration forms, and more

Though censorship issues arise in all types of settings, it can be useful to take a look through the lens of particular library types. This chapter compiles queries that illustrate the balancing act that takes place in our public libraries. Often librarians' work and parents' impulse to prioritize their own approach to their children's needs collide. To help librarians navigate such situations, Scales reminds us that the public library is a unique institution that is here "to serve the learning and educational needs of the entire community." At the same time, it is not appropriate for a public librarian to monitor what a child reads, as that is the caregiver's role. In so many instances, simply returning to these fundamentals, and educating parents about them, can be an effective way to resolve controversy over a chosen title. Underpinning this should be a transparent and consistent process that starts with the all-important materials reconsideration form. This simple document, and the process it represents, formalizes a complaint and takes the issue from a one-on-one conversation, which can be quite passionate, into a policy-based transparent process of reconsideration. Each step, however, is an opportunity to enrich the conversation around the role of the library.—*R. T. M.*

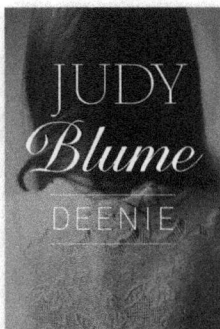

I'm the manager of a small branch of a large library system. I don't have a children's librarian on staff, but the children's librarians at the main library choose the books for the collection. A parent has filed a formal complaint that my staff allowed her nine-year-old daughter to check out *Deenie* (Bradbury, 1973) by Judy Blume. **How should I handle this?** *September 2013*

It sounds as if there are two issues:

- A problem with your staff
- A complaint against the book.

Make sure that the mother understands that it's never the role of the librarian to monitor what children read. Then invite the mother to file a book reconsideration form, which I assume is part of your library system's policy. *Deenie* is appropriate for most nine-year-olds. The mother needs to tell her daughter if she doesn't want her to read it. I do think it wise to ask the children's librarians at the main library to conduct a workshop in children's services for your staff. They may need reassurance about their roles.

৪৩ ◎ ଓଷ

I'm taking an online course in children's services from a university that is located in another part of the country. I have an issue with some of the theories about public library services to children. In my public library system, children are welcome to use the entire library collection. The professor defines children as birth to 11 years old. This makes me feel that I have to defend the policy of my library system. *September 2013*

Children should have free and open access to books and materials. Most children will reject what they aren't ready for, especially if they don't feel the materials are forbidden. What about 12- and 14-year-olds who simply want to continue using the children's room? Does this professor think that they should be banned because they grew up? Your library is on the right track.

৪৩ ◎ ଓଷ

An affluent private school requires its third graders to read Newbery books. In fact, it even has a contest to see who can read the most. Some parents have discovered that many of these award-winning titles are for much older readers, and they've challenged our public library for having books like Lois Lowry's *The Giver* (Houghton, 1993); Katherine Patterson's *Jacob, Have I Loved* (Crowell, 1980); and Cynthia Voigt's *Dicey's Song* (Atheneum, 1982) in our children's collection. What should we do? *March 2012*

First, I'd recommend that you inform the parents that your collection serves a wide age range of children and that the Newbery Medal may be awarded to books for "older" readers. Perhaps some of the parents have misunderstood the assignment. It's likely that the teachers have asked their students to read only age-appropriate Newbery winners. But if you discover that the parents are right, then it's a good idea to have a conversation with the teachers and review the list of Newbery Medal and Honor books with them, specifically highlighting the titles that are most likely to appeal to third graders. I suspect that the teachers haven't read all of these books, and they're simply trying to encourage kids to read quality literature. It sounds as though they need your guidance.

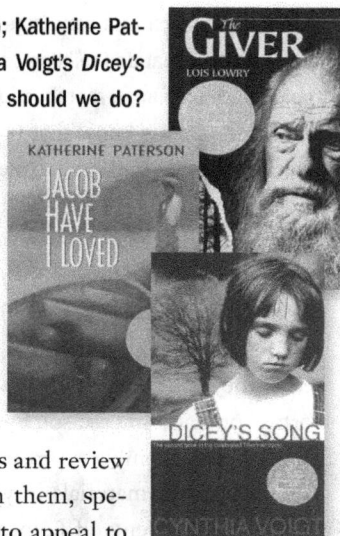

ℛ ◎ ঙ

I had a parent question why our public library has picture books on the Civil Rights Movement. He feels these books are inappropriate for young children, especially since our community is predominantly Caucasian. He wasn't satisfied with my explanation and plans to take his complaint to the library board. *August 2010*

I hope you told him that children of all ages need to know our nation's history, and that communities all across America, especially predominantly Caucasian ones, need to connect with that part of our history. Please explain to the library board and the patron that children study the Civil Rights Movement in American history classes and even our youngest children understand why we celebrate the birthday of Martin Luther King, Jr. Let them know that ignorance is far more frightening than knowledge. I have a hunch you're dealing with a bigoted patron. If that's the case, I hope your board is enlightened enough to recognize that. You might even suggest that the library begin making plans for Black History Month and include programming for the very young. Who knows? Maybe that patron will attend.

**I work in a branch of a very large public library system, and I don't know much about children's books. What do I tell homeschooling parents who object to us having books on certain topics, such as human reproduction, in our collection?** *January 2009*

Let those parents know that you're thrilled they use your library for their children's educational needs. Then, explain that the library's mission is to serve the learning and recreational reading needs of the entire community. Most public and many private schools teach human reproduction in science and health classes. And many parents turn to the library for materials to help them engage in good conversations about sex and sexuality with their children. The library is all about giving people choices. Although homeschooling parents can determine what their kids read and learn, they can't impose their views on others. Make sure to keep "reconsideration forms" on hand in case some homeschooling parents want to make a formal complaint. Just remember to treat them the same way you'd treat other patrons who complain about materials in your adult collection. If you still feel uncomfortable dealing with parents of homeschoolers, ask your director of children's services to visit your branch and offer an appropriate workshop for you and your colleagues. An opportunity to do a little role-playing may help you feel more comfortable.

෨ ◎ ඃ

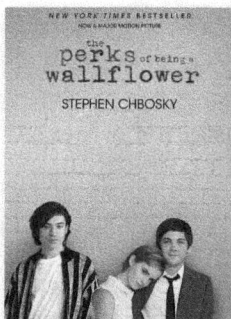

**I'm a teen librarian in a large public library system. We're having so many book challenges that we need a full-time librarian just to handle the cases. I believe that teen books have gotten too edgy, and I'm uncomfortable with some of the books in our collection, like *The Perks of Being a Wallflower* (MTV, 1999). I don't want to be guilty of censorship, but I think some teen books really belong in our adult section. How should I deal with these edgy books?** *July 2009*

*The Perks of Being a Wallflower* is a young adult novel, and therefore, it belongs in the teen section. I don't know what other teen titles concern you, but I hope that you and your colleagues are reading the books and not making judgments based on the flap copy. You may not personally like some of the books in your teen collection, but you need to separate your personal values from your professional decisions. Dealing with book challenges can take a lot of time, but procedures must be followed. That's part of a librarian's job description.

෨ ◎ ඃ

I handle all of the collection development for a very small community library. My library director has told me to stop purchasing graphic novels. Plus, he says he's going to move these titles from the children's room to the adult section. When I asked him what prompted his decision, he just said, "A library isn't about comic books." I always thought our community was fairly liberal. Plus, I purchased graphic novels because our kids were asking for them. **What should I do?** *May 2009*

I would recommend asking your library director the following questions: Has he received a specific complaint? Does he think that graphic novels are "comic books"? And if that's the case, what's wrong with comic books? How does he plan to explain to young readers the sudden disappearance of an entire collection of popular titles? My guess is that he hasn't thought these things through, and he's simply responding to one loud citizen.

Here are some things you can do: first, introduce your director to a few graphic novels of exceptional literary merit. Next, suggest that the library sponsor a program about children's literature for parents. Let your young patrons do the teaching. Make sure to invite all types of young readers to take part in the session, including kids who are attracted to graphic novels. Even parents who are likely to complain about graphic novels will beam if their child is invited to participate.

Just remember that the only way to solve a problem is to talk about it. When such talks happen openly and publicly, then everyone is a winner.

ಐ ◎ ಚಿ

A parent of a fourth grader recently asked if it was appropriate to have Judy Blume's *Blubber* (Bradbury, 1974) in our collection. I was totally shocked. Why are people still getting riled up over that book? *March 2008*

*Blubber* has long been one of Judy Blume's most challenged books. Some parents just don't like the way "the kids treat one another" in the story. Blume's book is a popular read with elementary school students because she understands what it's really like to be 10 years old and the target of bullies. My guess is that the parent has heard about the novel but hasn't read it.

Has the parent filed a formal complaint? If she has, then simply let the process run its course—odds are, your reconsideration committee will vote to retain the book. If the parent hasn't filed a complaint, I'd use this as an opportunity to help her understand

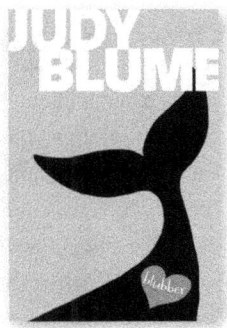

how *Blubber* may help kids be less inclined to bully or tease their peers. You can even suggest specific themes that the parent could use to discuss the book with her child. That approach allows everyone to win.

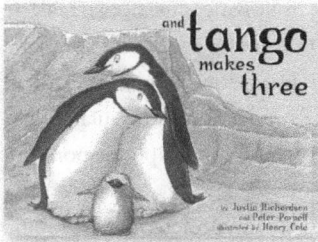

ဢ ◎ ଔ

**My public library director has asked us to move *And Tango Makes Three* (Simon & Schuster, 2005) from the picture-book section to our nonfiction section. Is that a form of censorship?** *July 2007*

It's certainly an attempt to restrict access to the book. *And Tango Makes Three* should be housed where young children can easily access it. Though young readers have a natural interest in nonfiction, they don't always gravitate to that section of the library without guidance. It usually takes a parent or a librarian to lead children to the nonfiction books related to their particular interests. The children in your public library are in luck if they happen to love animals, especially penguins. I recommend that you meet with your director and ask her to reconsider her request. [Editor's note: Though the authors of *And Tango Makes Three* acknowledge that the story is based on a true incident, the Library of Congress CIP data for *And Tango Makes Three* classifies this picture book as a work of fiction.]

ဢ ◎ ଔ

**A couple of grown-ups were recently in our public library's children's room putting bookmarks in some of our books. When I asked if I could help them, they fled. It turns out they had put bookmarks with a Christian message in a number of fairy tales, scary stories, and nonfiction works about witchcraft and vampires. What do you think they were up to?** *November 2007*

They may have been part of an organized group. The couple probably had a list of specific titles and subjects to look for. There's no way you can really know what they were up to unless they lodge a formal challenge. Since they fled, they're probably trying to intimidate the staff. Make sure your colleagues are prepared to deal with future incidents like this. For starters, you should remove the bookmarks immediately. The last thing you want to happen is for children to feel threatened about their reading choices. I'm a fan of being as proactive as possible, so I'd encourage you to set up an information session for parents: tell them about their children's rights and the many services you offer youngsters. You might also schedule an open house in the children's room and encourage families to browse the collection. That's a great way to familiarize parents and children with your entire collection and gain support for the library. Finally, ask your young patrons if they'd like to adopt a specific section of the collection. Then, booktalk some of those titles.

# 7

# *Confronting Censorship in School Libraries and Classrooms*

### Educating teachers, connecting to curriculum, and providing the all-important element of interest

Just as public libraries are unique so are school libraries. And, more distinctions emerge depending on whether a school is public or private. This chapter captures a range of confrontational moments, including several that arise from the anticipation of trouble instead of any actual trouble. This speaks to the ongoing chilling effect of the censors in our culture. "Do not cave!" is Scales' resounding charge to one school librarian whose fatigue with challenges threatens to undermine her resolve. Instead, Scales emphasizes a need to understand the library's link to curriculum and the rights of students in private vs. public settings. Bolstered by policy and past practice, librarians can focus on creating a culture that fosters the freedom to read over the fear of the wrong book at the wrong time. And teachers and kids will get the critical support they so desperately need.—*R. T. M.*

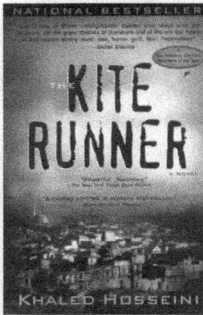

A science teacher in my high school is doing homebound teaching for a 10th grader who is enrolled in a global studies class that is reading Khaled Hosseini's *The Kite Runner* (Riverhead, 2003). The teacher is uncomfortable discussing the book because of its content. The girl's parents haven't complained. *November 2014*

If the teacher cannot guide the student with the assignments that teachers have provided, then the school needs to find another teacher. Perhaps the global studies teacher would be willing to visit the student, or call or email her, to engage her in discussion. My bet is that the teacher hasn't read the book but has heard about it and doesn't know how to guide the student.

ജ © ര

I work in a private K–12 girls school that serves an international population. I recently recommended Louisa May Alcott's 19th century "classic" *Little Women* to a sixth grader. The girl did an oral book report on the novel in class. The teacher, who isn't Christian, complained to me because she didn't like the Christmas scene in the book. I was left speechless. How do I respond? *April 2014*

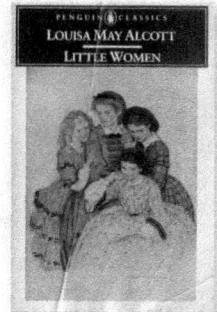

The story is about the March family, and they just happen to celebrate Christmas. This doesn't mean that everyone who reads the book is Christian. Ask the teacher how she would feel if a student reported on a book set during Rosh Hashanah or Ramadan. I would hope she'd engage students in conversation about religious or secular observances in their families. This seems especially appropriate for a school that serves an international population. You aren't promoting Christianity by recommending *Little Women*. Neither is a reader by reporting on it.

ജ © ര

I'm a librarian in a high school with a student body of 2,500. Many of our girls belong to sororities. The school doesn't sanction these organizations, and some of the behaviors generated by rush create issues at school. Last fall, the girls had a contest to see who could lose the most weight. This prompted uproar among parents, and they have requested that we ban books that deal with eating disorders in the library. One of the books they spe-

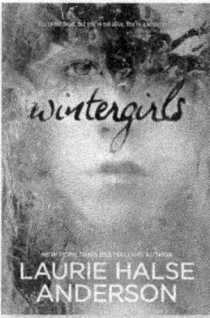

**cifically wanted removed is Laurie Halse Anderson's** *Wintergirls* **(Viking, 2009).** *April 2014*

I can't think of a book that promotes eating disorders, but I can think of many that ask teens to think about the health risks. One of those books is *Wintergirls*, and I wish the sorority girls would take the time to read it. Do not remove any book from the library just because parents have requested it. Tell them they can file a formal challenge, and then let the process work. Speak with the school administration and counselor, and suggest that the school sponsor a series of eating disorder workshops for parents and their daughters. There are health professionals who'd volunteer their time to work with the groups. Perhaps you could lead a mother-daughter book club and focus on books that deal with eating disorders. Let the parents know that some of the most important books are ones that give pause. These proactive measures may save the books and the girls.

ॐ ◎ ॐ

**I teach freshman Honors and Pre-AP English in a college preparatory school. A parent recently challenged** *The Catcher in the Rye* **(Little, Brown, 1951) because she didn't think it appropriate for ninth grade. Do you have any current materials or articles with which to retort these types of challenges?** *February 2014*

*The Catcher in the Rye* is commonly taught in ninth grade, and is one of the most challenged books in classrooms and libraries. The National Council of Teachers of English (NCTE) offers advice and justification for teaching challenged books. One publication highly recommended on this site is Rationales for Teaching Challenged Books, a CD-ROM published jointly by NCTE and the International Reading Association (IRA). I also recommend the current edition of The Students' Right to Read, from NCTE. The National Coalition Against Censorship (NCAC) offers a First Amendment in Schools Toolkit for schools. *Keep Them Reading: An Anti-Censorship Handbook for Educators* (Teachers College Press) by ReLeah Cossett Lent and Gloria Pipkin, two practitioners with experience dealing with censorship in the classroom, should give teachers courage as they deal with similar battles (see addendum, p. 138).

I'm an elementary school librarian and have once again been hit with a challenge to Barbara Parks' "Junie B. Jones" series. The specific complaint is "disorderly conduct" and the grammar in the books. I'm tired of the challenges. I fear that I'm about to cave. *July 2013*

Do not cave! The purpose of a library is to serve all students. This doesn't mean that everything in the collection satisfies every child or every parent. The way to solve the problem isn't to remove the books, but to help children see that the "disorderly conduct" and the "bad grammar" define the character of Junie B. Jones—and contribute to the humor. Turn the discussion into an English lesson by asking them to correct the grammar. Children read these books to be entertained and don't necessarily emulate the character. Trust their intelligence.

೧೦ ◎ ೧೪

I had no problems with Suzanne Collins' *The Hunger Games* (Scholastic, 2008) in my middle school library until the movie was released. A parent who hasn't read the book took her son to see the movie and she was bothered by the content. She called me because she doesn't think the book should be in a middle school library. She added that neither the movie nor the book disturb, her son, and that makes her nervous. Help! *July 2013*

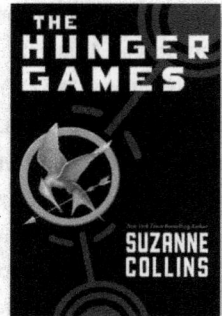

Tell her that the book is appropriate for middle school students, and that it was selected for the library based on reviews. Share the reviews with her and ask her to consider reading the book. Encourage her to discuss it with her son and ask him to reflect on its powerful themes. Sometimes conversation solves a disagreement. She needs to understand that she can guide what her son reads, but she doesn't have the right to guide what other children read. Let the complaint go through a formal process if the mother isn't satisfied.

೧೦ ◎ ೧೪

**A group of parents appeared at the school board meeting and insisted that we remove all fairy tales from our elementary schools. Their complaint was that the violence and magic in most of these tales promote evil behavior. What should I do?** *May 2012*

You didn't tell me how the school board responded. I hope it had the good sense to let the parents know that fairy tales are classics, and their children will eventually have to call upon their knowledge of these tales when they're referred to in other literature. Maybe you need to have a parent session and expose them to the many versions of popular fairy tales. I bet that will solve your problem.

80 ◎ ⊙ℛ

**My district offers eighth graders the option of taking ninth-grade honors English. Parents want their "accelerated" students in the class, but they don't want them exposed to some of the required readings, such as** *Romeo and Juliet.* **The teacher is frustrated because she's expected to teach the prescribed ninth-grade curriculum. What should I tell her?** *May 2012*

Teach the curriculum. The parents have the option of taking their kids out of the class. If they want them "accelerated," they have to accept all that goes with it.

80 ◎ ⊙ℛ

**Our new elementary school principal, who comes from a fairly conservative private school, doesn't want our library to have any banned titles. He recently told me that he'd personally check our catalog to make sure that there weren't any titles on the banned books list. Since our district doesn't have a library coordinator, I feel like I don't have an advocate. Fortunately, our district has a selection policy and reconsideration guidelines. What should I do?** *January 2012*

Perhaps the principal doesn't realize that public schools have different standards and mission statements than many private schools. Give him a copy of your district's policy so he can become familiar with the proper guidelines for dealing with book challenges. Explain to him that a challenge must be filed and brought before a committee before a book may be removed from the library, and that he's welcome to register a challenge. He also needs to know that a separate form must be completed for each title that's challenged. The idea of going through that time-consuming process may quickly change his mind.

I know it can be intimidating when you feel like you don't have an advocate. But just remember to stick to your district's policy. Your principal should be required to jump through the same hoops as anyone else who wishes to challenge materials. If he accuses you of insubordination, then go to the superintendent or your principal's superior and simply let that person know that you're following the district's policy. That's why we have policies. Let me know what happens.

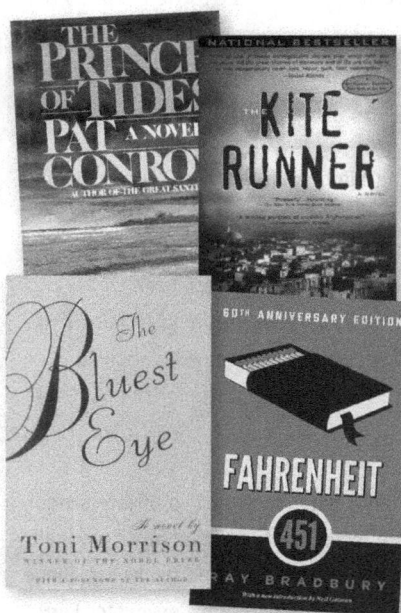

℘ ◎ ଓ

In the last three years, we've had to deal with a number of challenges to novels that are used in our high school's AP English class, including Khaled Hosseini's *The Kite Runner* (Riverhead, 2003), Pat Conroy's *The Prince of Tides* (Houghton Mifflin, 1986), Toni Morrison's *The Bluest Eye* (Holt, 1970), and Ray Bradbury's *Fahrenheit 451* (Simon & Schuster, 1967). Although all of these books have ultimately been retained, it's time consuming to deal with these challenges year after year. Do you have any suggestions? *January 2012*

According to a person I spoke to at the National Council of Teachers of English, high school students enroll in AP English classes to earn college credit, so they must be held to the same expectations as college freshmen. If high school students or their parents don't approve of the teacher's literature choices, they can always drop the class. This option needs to be made perfectly clear to students and parents at the beginning of the school year. Include that message on the syllabus, explain it to students on the first day of class, and make sure that their parents understand this when you meet them during an open house. This gives kids plenty of time to opt out of the class before the grading period has begun.

℘ ◎ ଓ

A substitute teacher told one of our fourth graders that Jeff Kinney's *Diary of a Wimpy Kid* (Amulet, 2007) wasn't an appropriate book for him because she saw it in a local bookstore's young adult section. The student's mother called me and asked me to explain the situation. This isn't the first time I've had to deal with this issue. I blame the bookstore for this grief. What would you recommend? *January 2011*

Did the mother complain about the substitute teacher or the book? I hope she complained about the former, because the book is quite popular with fourth graders. I've been in bookstores where they've shelved any book with chapters in the young adult section. This simply tells me that they don't know much about the books. Here's what I'd recommend saying to the mother: "I bought the 'Diary of a Wimpy Kid' series for our school library because I know how much our students love these books. The bookstore doesn't classify them in the same way we do."

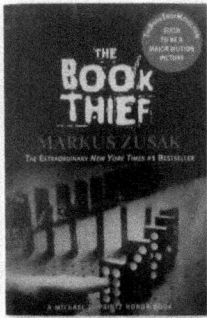

ℬ ◎ ℭ

I bought Markus Zusak's *The Book Thief* (Knopf, 2006) for our middle school library. A friend told me that her adult book club had read it, and she couldn't understand why a middle school library would have the book in its collection. Now I'm afraid someone is going to challenge it. Did I make a mistake? *January 2011*

You made a professional judgment—now stick to it. Explain to your friend why you chose the title. I know many middle school students who have read the novel and can speak passionately about it. And I know teachers who have used it successfully when teaching units on the Holocaust. Perhaps your friend and her book club underestimate the ability of middle school students.

ℬ ◎ ℭ

My son's middle school teacher won't allow him to do a report on Chris Crutcher's *Angry Management* (Greenwillow, 2009) because she finds the book offensive. I'm a middle school librarian (at another school), and I recommended the book to my son in the first place. What should I do? *November 2011*

I bet the teacher hasn't even read it. She's probably aware that *Angry Management* has been removed from summer reading lists in some parts of the country. I'd call the teacher and tell her that you recommended the book to your son. You might remind her that someone might be offended by some of the titles that she's teaching. It's important that we know that free expression is two-sided.

ℵ ◎ ℜ

**One of our parents returned from a religious retreat with a 10-page list of books that elementary school children shouldn't read. When she asked me to remove them from the library, I said, "No." Now I'm afraid she'll rally other parents behind her. What should I do?** *March 2011*
Good for you for standing up to her. Now, don't worry about it until something happens. Here are some things you can do to prepare for a potential problem:

Prepare (in your head) what to say to parents who question certain books in your collection. For example, you might want to say, "Libraries are about choice" or "We must serve the needs of all students."
If you haven't already, read every book on her list. It's difficult to defend books you don't know. And, they're sure to be interesting reading.

- ◎ Look up reviews for each book and file them, for easy access should you need them.

- ◎ Review your school district's materials-review policy.

- ◎ Have reconsideration forms available for parents who want to make a formal challenge; remember, they must fill out a form for each challenged book.

- ◎ Inform your principal of the steps that you've taken to prepare for a mass challenge

ℵ ◎ ℜ

**A parent who objected to one of the titles in an eighth-grade classroom collection has recruited a group of parents to search for other "objectionable" titles in the teacher's collection. I'm the school's librarian, and I'm afraid those parents may be heading my way next.** *May 2009*
Let's deal with the classroom situation first. No parent should be allowed to paw through a teacher's classroom for any reason. Where was the school administrator? There should be a reconsideration policy in place for classroom libraries. If your school or district doesn't have one, I'd encourage the school board to develop one. Then a parent who objects to a book has a stated path to follow.

Now, let's examine your fears regarding the same thing happening in the library.

No library is immune from parents who are on a witch hunt. Express your fears to your principal, and let her know that you need her support. If parents show up in the library, let them know that they need to make an appointment so that you have time to spend with them. If they say they just want to look around, simply tell them that this isn't a convenient time because you're expecting a class. By the way, I can't imagine that there's any school nowadays that allows parents to roam the building unannounced. I would hope that the library is locked after school hours. If not, now's the time to begin locking it.

Just a reminder: Do you have a selection policy? What about a reconsideration policy? Is there a policy regarding visitors in the school and library? These policies are your best protection.

૭ ◎ ೞ

**A teacher in my school wants me to remove *Tar Beach* (Crown, 1991), a Caldecott Honor book by Faith Ringgold. She objects to the book because the protagonist's family picnics on the roof of an apartment building. In the teacher's mind, that's a safety hazard, and she's worried that students who read the book may do the same thing. What do I tell her?** *March 2008*
If this teacher's reasoning wasn't so ludicrous, I'd find this funny. The first thing I'd tell her is that the roof may be the only place where some urban children can picnic. Then, I'd tell the teacher that kids don't emulate everything they read. *Tar Beach* (Crown, 1991) is a terrific book about people coming together to confront social injustice. The book broadens students' sensitivities—and for that reason, it's an important story. Finally, I would remind the teacher that she can formally challenge the book, but my bet is she won't. She's probably just trying to rattle your chain.

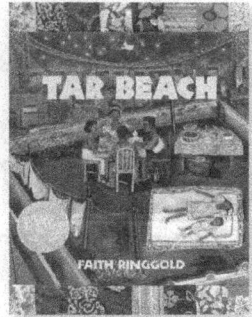

૭ ◎ ೞ

**During a mandatory workshop for media specialists, our superintendent told us that a group of "concerned citizens" had come to him with a long list of titles that they thought didn't belong in school libraries. He assured them that none of his media specialists would ever purchase anything controversial. The superintendent never told us what books were on the list, but his tone suggested that we'd better watch our step. His message upset and frightened many of my**

colleagues. Should we ask to see the list, so we can avoid those titles? *November 2008*

The superintendent's message obviously caught your colleagues off guard or I'm sure they would have realized that this was a good opportunity to talk about your materials selection and review policies. I'd invite the superintendent to attend the next districtwide meeting of media specialists. This time be prepared to discuss your policies, and let him know that the term "controversial" is ambiguous. Some parents feel that every work of fantasy is "evil." Others don't want their children reading about bullies, family conflicts, death, or boy-girl relationships. Some even object to the grammar in the "Junie B. Jones" series (Random House), the underwear in the "Captain Underpants" series (Scholastic), and the humor in books like *Harriet the Spy* (Harper & Row), and *Amelia Bedelia* (HarperCollins).

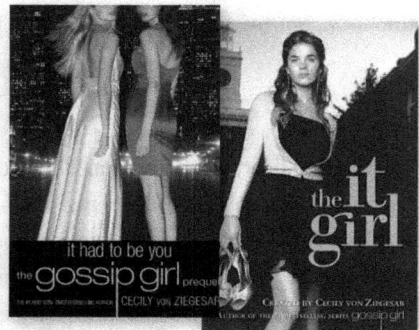

Don't ask to see the group's list unless you're curious. I bet it's one of those lists that's traveling across the Internet like wildfire. That's how these organized groups often work. Purging titles from library collections is an act of censorship. Don't give in to bullies. Instead, put up your dukes and fight them with knowledge, confidence, and wise policies.

ဆ ◎ ର

I'm a second-year librarian at a Catholic high school. Last week, my principal demanded that I remove both the *Gossip Girl* (Little Brown) and *It Girl* (Little Brown) series books from our shelves. I was worried that I'd be placed on probation or lose my job if I denied his request. He has no qualms about defending other books with "questionable" content, if they're being taught by a teacher who can hold her students' hands through the difficult passages. I feel like I caved in by removing the books. What should I have done? *March 2008*

Under the circumstances, I think you did the only thing that you could have done. Even the most radical free-speech proponents would never suggest that librarians do anything that would cause them to lose their jobs. It's too bad that your principal doesn't recognize that high school students need access to popular fiction for recreational reading. My guess is that he doesn't feel these series promote the Christian values purported by the Catholic diocese. Remember, private school students don't have the same First Amendment protection that public school students have. Since you're in a parochial school, I doubt you'll ever convince your principal of the value of these series. When students ask for the "Gossip Girl" series or the "It Girl" series books, you can direct them to the local public library.

80 ◎ ca

I've discovered that my Catholic high school doesn't have a selection-and-retention policy for library materials. I haven't had any luck finding examples of other private schools' policies. What's your advice? *March 2008*

Every school needs a selection-and-retention policy. Policies for public school libraries will look very different than those of private or parochial schools. Check with the Catholic Library Association (www.cathla.org); they may have some sample policies you can look at. If not, perhaps they can put you in touch with other Catholic schools that have policies. In any event, consider forming a committee of students, teachers, and parents to help write a policy. Who knows? Maybe in the process of developing one, students may actually plead for more popular fiction in your collection. And if you're lucky, the school board will listen. That's the best defense against your principal removing popular books in the future.

80 ◎ ca

What do you think of Joyce Carol Oates's books? Should they be censored in school libraries? *January 2008*

The word censored makes me twinge. I assume you're talking about a high school library, which should offer a wide range of adult and young adult titles. If your school or district has a selection policy and Oates's books meet its guidelines, then there shouldn't be a question about the appropriateness of her books in your library. Most middle school students aren't ready for Oates, and I doubt that they'd even care if her titles were available. They have other adolescent concerns and interests on their minds. My high school students, on the other hand, liked Oates's works, so I included them in our collection.

Remember that libraries are about choice. That's the message that we should always deliver to students, parents, and school officials.

ℬ ◎ ℛ

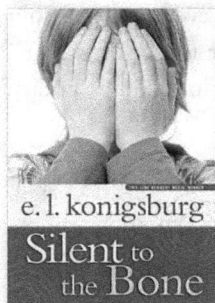

At a nearby middle school, a parent has challenged E. L. Konigsburg's *Silent to the Bone* (Atheneum, 2000) because of its sexual content. I'm a middle school librarian, and although I haven't read the book, it's in our collection. I'm worried: What should I do if parents begin asking me why we offer the novel? *January 2008*

You should start by reading the book. It's very difficult to defend a title you haven't read. Of course, no librarian can read every title in their library, but I think it's wise to read any book that has been challenged in a nearby school district. Censors have a way of spreading the word, and the media loves to help them. *Silent to the Bone* is an intriguing story that most middle-school students love. I suggest that you ask your students to read the book, and lead them in a discussion of it.

ℬ ◎ ℛ

Our superintendent has removed Justin Richardson and Peter Parnell's *And Tango Makes Three* (Simon & Schuster, 2005) from our library. He had heard that the picture book, which tells the story of a same-sex penguin couple and their child, had been challenged by some school and public libraries. Since nobody in our district has questioned the book's content, is the superintendent's response appropriate? *July 2007*

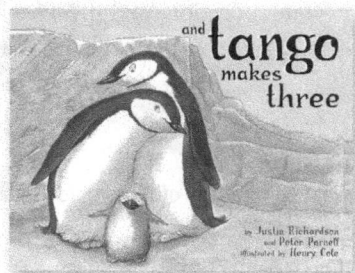

No, his actions aren't appropriate. There's a good chance that the book will be embraced by your students and parents. They should be given that opportunity. See *Board of Education* v. *Pico*, a 1982 case in which the Supreme Court ruled that school officials may not remove titles from school libraries simply because they disagree with the book's content or ideas.

ℒ ◎ ℛ

**I recently read a news story about a 15-year-old who refused to return a school library book. She and her grandmother didn't think it was appropriate for high school students. I'm worried that this story may cause similar problems in our school or community. Is that kind of behavior common?** *November 2007*

Yes, it's a common form of censorship. In some states, refusing to return a library book is considered stealing, and it's a misdemeanor. The student and her grandmother are taking matters into their own hands to avoid going through a formal reconsideration process. I'm sure that the case will eventually fall into the hands of the school administration, which will put pressure on the two to return the book. In the meantime, I'd suggest you rush out and purchase another copy of the book. Since the story made the local newspaper, students will probably be lining up to read the book. It's always possible that someone will see the story and search your collection for the book in question. I suspect the title you're referring to is Ellen Wittlinger's *Sandpiper* (Simon & Schuster, 2005), which was removed from a high school library in Tuscaloosa, AL. I'd encourage you to share the news story with your students and booktalk the novel. After they've had a chance to read it, discuss the case with them. That way, you're letting them know that you respect their opinions. Students should also be informed of the district's reconsideration policy.

ℒ ◎ ℛ

**Copies of *The Perks of Being a Wallflower* by Stephen Chbosky (Pocket Books, 1999) were removed from elementary school libraries in Apache Junction, AZ. Is the school district guilty of censorship?** *September 2006*

My answer is an emphatic no. *The Perks of Being a Wallflower* is an excellent novel for young adult readers, but it's not appropriate for elementary-school-age children (even though it has a fourth-grade reading level). There are more and more censorship cases developing across the nation because educators are relying on computerized programs to select books.

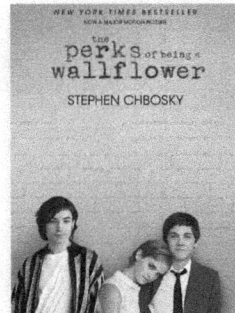

But students' maturity levels and reading levels aren't the same. Also, sometimes we must be willing to admit that we've made a mistake in selecting a title. That's why it's important when reading reviews to note the age group for which a book is recommended.

I've heard that some high schools are reexamining *The Perks of Being a Wallflower* because of what happened in Arizona. That's too bad, because older students deserve to have access to it. If the novel is removed from the state's high school libraries without a formal challenge, and without due process, then censorship has occurred. School administrators should be reminded of *Island Trees Union School District No. 26* vs. *Pico*, a case in which the Supreme Court ruled that books could be removed from school libraries only if they were "educationally unsuitable."

# 8

# *Library Programs, Displays, and Censorship*

## Misunderstanding Banned Books Week, and the role of fairy tales

The arm of the censor extends well beyond book selection and use. Librarians confront restrictive efforts as they plan events and programs and in the daily use of materials in displays they use to market the collection. And, often, the censor is within. This chapter gathers some shocking examples of how fear of controversy leads to censorship from within our institutions. Principals, teachers, and other librarians introduce limitations even as they try to dodge public conflicts. Such self-censorship is one of the most troubling themes in Scales' work. To correct these situations, Scales offers information. Information about the background of, for instance, Banned Books Week can help calm an anxious teacher. Information about, in another case, the riches of Mother Goose can offset a principal's worry about violence in those stories. Instance by instance, the librarian gains strength through sharing information over giving in to limitations brought by fear.—*R. T. M.*

**A language arts teacher and I have received a grant for a visiting writer. The author we would like to ask has a book that has been challenged in another state. My principal wants us to ask the writer not to mention that book in her presentation.** *November 2014*

To ask a writer not to speak about a controversial book is an abridgement of free speech. Just because a book has been challenged in another state doesn't mean it will be challenged in your school. The smartest thing to do is to use the title with students and focus on the book as a whole. Ask them their thoughts about the challenged part. Students of all ages like to know that their opinion counts.

Another approach is to have a group of parents read the book and lead small group discussions with students. This may require a training session with parents so that they understand how to lead an open discussion with students. Maybe your principal will have a change of mind if parents are involved. What do you think students learn if they ask the writer about the title, and the writer says that she's not allowed to talk about it?

ℬ ◎ ℭ

**I'm a middle school librarian and am always seeking new programming ideas. This year, I decided to develop programming centered on the national observance of Red Ribbon Week, Bullying Awareness Month, Mental Illness Month, etc. I had an incredible planning session with teachers. Our ideas included a display of books and materials that deal with these specific issues. Then the principal told me that such observances have no place in middle school. He doesn't want the community to think that the school has a drug or bullying problem.** *November 2013*

Most communities celebrate such awareness campaigns. Talk to community leaders and ask them to work with the school district to develop programs that communicate such issues to students. I doubt that the school district will say "no" to these leaders. Let the principal know that creating awareness doesn't mean that the school has a problem, but the school does have a problem if it doesn't help students understand these social issues. Maybe the kids are being bullied and don't know how to report it. Perhaps drugs are a problem where they live and they are too frightened to tell anyone. Through awareness campaigns, students learn where to go for help. Schools have the responsibility to protect children. The best protection is through information and awareness.

ℬ ◎ ℭ

A children's librarian in a small public library, I announced a month-long storytelling festival for school-age children. A parent of a third grader complained that the program involves fairy tales. I'm worried that the library director will ask me to pull the program. What should I do? *July 2013*

One parent shouldn't be allowed to dictate a program. I suggest that you try to reason with her about the value of fairy tales. If she insists that her daughter isn't to take part, then that is her choice. Let the director know that fairy tales are a large part of the oral tradition, and that no one else has complained. It should be treated in the same way as a book challenge. A formal complaint process solves the issue most of the time.

໑ ◎ ଔ

A teacher in our school saw a Banned Books Week display at the public library that included William Steig's *Abel's Island* (Farrar, Straus and Giroux, 1976). She reads that book to her fourth graders every year and was concerned that she'd have problems if parents happened to see the display. How can I assure the teacher that she has nothing to worry about? *January 2013*

The purpose of a Banned Books Week display is to celebrate the freedom to read, and to create an awareness of challenges to that freedom. Teachers shouldn't allow those displays to frighten them. According to the American Library Association, the only public challenge to *Abel's Island* was in Clay County, FL, in 1990. The novel was removed from the optional reading lists for fifth and sixth graders because of "references to drinking wine which the administrators determined violated the district's substance abuse policy."

Just because parents may have seen the display doesn't mean they'll bring a challenge. The teacher has successfully used the book in the past, and she should continue to use it. Let her know that you are behind her, and that her former students' enjoyment of the book should be testament that she makes good reading choices.

໑ ◎ ଔ

A local church recently asked me to display a brochure about its vacation Bible school in our public school library. I refused because that would violate the separation between church and state. Our principal attends the church, and some of its members have complained to him. Now I'm on the hot seat. *July 2012*

You are absolutely right to refuse to display the pamphlet. I'd expect a public school principal to understand this issue. Check your district's policies: I bet they prohibit displaying religious promotional materials in school.

&#8485; ◎ ᙂ

There's a child who never misses any of our small public library's weekly storytimes. The problem is, her mother sits nearby and occasionally makes comments while I'm reading, which makes me nervous since she's challenged some of our books. She's starting to affect my selections for storytime. *July 2012*

Tell the mother that it's terrific that she brings her child to storytime, but ask if she can busy herself in another part of the library during the program. You can simply say that sometimes having another adult in the room inhibits the way that kids respond to the story. You might also let her know ahead of time what book you're planning to read, so she can decide if she wants her child to hear it. Also, offer her a volunteer job, such as shelving books or preparing materials for a special activity. If she becomes more involved in your program, she may see things differently. You are the professional. Do not let her dictate what you read.

&#8485; ◎ ᙂ

Our public library is teaming up with the school district to sponsor a family literacy day. We plan to invite writers for kids of all ages. I'm on the planning committee, and I have to admit that we're frightened after reading about the fiasco in Humble, TX. What's your advice? *November 2010*

As many readers know, this incident has received wide-spread coverage. After a middle school librarian and a small group of parents complained about Ellen Hopkins's works, Humble's superintendent of schools withdrew the author's invitation to its Teen Lit Festival. In a show of solidarity, four writers refused to appear at the event and the superintendent cancelled it. This was very unfortunate for all concerned, but the biggest losers were Humble's students, whose free speech rights were stripped right out from under them. Please don't let this situation scare you. Instead, take courage and forge straight ahead with your plans. Begin now by getting members of your community involved. Present your plans at meetings of civic groups, the PTA, and friends of the library. To further publicize the day, ask for volunteers to read the visiting authors' books beforehand. The more people who buy into your event, the more successful it will be. Display the featured titles in your public library's branches and in the school libraries. Invite senior citizens to read the works aloud to young children. This type of involvement will truly turn your plan into a community event. You won't have any problems because you'll have so many people behind you.

80 ◎ ଔ

I recently read Edward Lear's *The Owl and the Pussycat* to a first-grade class that giggled every time I said the word pussycat. Their teacher told me I should've quit reading the poem because of the word pussy. Have things gotten so bad in schools that we can't even read aloud classic poetry? *August 2010*

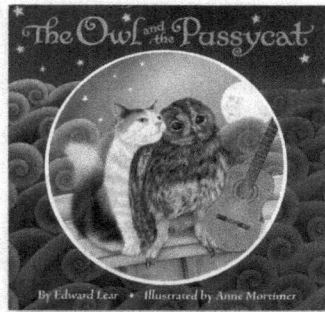

I'm so happy that you read the poem aloud, and I hope you'll continue to do that. Too many children don't know this particular poem because adults don't want to deal with the word pussy. The poem is great fun, and I bet that your students can be taught to laugh for all the right reasons. They are halfway there, because they've got a librarian who's willing to take them there. Invite the teacher to observe when you explain the meaning of the word pussy.

80 ◎ ଔ

I'm a second-year elementary school librarian. I love working with the faculty and students, but working with the administration is a challenge. The principal comes in every day and asks what I'm doing with the students. I feel as though he's watching over my shoulder. One day he walked in while I was playing a Mother Goose trivia game with the students. He told me that he didn't think that I should be using Mother Goose rhymes because they're too violent. Another time, he said I shouldn't use fairy tales. What should I do? *November 2010*

It's time to sit down with your principal and ask him to share his concerns. Maybe a parent has voiced a complaint or he's dealt with one who's opposed to those genres. If that's the case, ask him to let you deal directly with that parent. Also, invite the principal to take part in the trivia game. He may discover how much fun he can have in the library. Those who oppose fairy tales are often so busy fussing about the "evil" in them they fail to see that good usually triumphs in the stories. By the time they're in elementary school, students should be beyond the Disney versions of their favorite fairy tales. In fact, invite the principal to hear your students discuss the differences between the original versions of *Cinderella* or *Snow White* and the Disney adaptations. I bet he'll be blown away by their observations.

৩ ◎ ೧

**I'd love to celebrate Banned Books Week with my elementary school students, but it's tough to find activities that are geared toward kids that age. Can you suggest some?** *September 2008* It's difficult for students who haven't studied our Constitution or grasped the idea of freedom to understand the concept of Banned Books Week. Here are a few suggestions:

◎ With the youngest children, ask them to recite a few familiar Mother Goose rhymes. Tell them that some people thinkkids shouldn't read those rhymes. Then read aloud "Peter, Peter, Pumpkin Eater," "There Was an Old Woman Who Lived in a Shoe," "Tom, Tom, the Piper's Son," and "Humpty Dumpty." Have your class brainstorm the reasons why some people may object to them. Explain that in our country we have the freedom to read these rhymes or anything else we choose. Point out that what students read is between them and their parents.

◎ Ask your students to draw a picture of "freedom." Then have them add the title or a picture of their favorite book to their drawings. Discuss the reasons why you asked them to do that.

◎ Encourage kids to name a book that they've never finished. Why did they stop reading it? Did they find the book boring? Was there something that offended them? During the discussion, let students know that their opinions count. Explain that every reader is different. Some like fantasies, others like realistic stories. Many readers prefer nonfiction, and some crave historical novels. That's why libraries need to offer many different kinds of books. Talk about the phrase "freedom to read." Discuss the connection between the freedom to read and the freedom to stop reading a book they simply don't enjoy.

◎ Display some of your upper-elementary-school students' favorite books that have been challenged, such as E. B. White's *Charlotte's Web* (Harper, 1952), Shel Silverstein's *Where the Sidewalk Ends* (Harper, 1974), Louis Sacher's *Holes* (Farrar, Straus and Giroux, 1998), Avi's *The True Confessions of Charlotte Doyle* (Orchard Books, 1990), and *Bridge to Terabithia* (Crowell, 1997). Have your students pretend they're having a conversation with someone who thinks they shouldn't read those books. What might they say to that person?

# 9

# *Filtering, Digital Access, Cyberbullying*

## Reality check in an online world

Intentional or inadvertent, censorship also plays out in our increasingly online world. Librarians have been walking the line since even before the early days of the Children's Internet Protection Act. They strive to increase access by closing the digital divide and by working to limit the impact of overzealous filtering programs. And, they have a role in moving policy forward around the use of social media and other blocked resources. As these entries illustrate, librarians also work to create an online environment that is inclusive and vibrant by raising awareness of cyberbullying. The themes that surface here point to the important work that is so essential to ensure an online world that supports and protects real access for people at every age. —*R. T. M.*

A parent of a middle schooler has complained that her son can't complete a social studies assignment because our district's computers have such strict Internet filters. The boy's father lost his job, and the family can't afford to have a home computer—so the student depends on ours to complete many of his assignments. What should I do? *April 2013*

Unfortunately, strict Internet filtering is the reality in many schools. Check your district's Internet Use Policy and make sure there's a provision to unblock sites that students may need. Perhaps you could meet with other teachers and see which sites kids will need to complete their upcoming assignments. Then ask the IT person to unblock them in advance.

ෆ ◎ �

My school district is adamant that our students must meet the Common Core standards for reading and literature. I'm especially concerned about the "Production and Distribution of Writing" standard, which requires kids to "Use technology, including the Internet, to produce and publish writing as well as to interact and collaborate with others." Our school's computers are heavily filtered, and the district's policy doesn't allow students to use email or social media during the school day. *April 2013*

Schedule a meeting with those who have the power to change the policy, including members of the IT department. Point out that this particular standard is impossible for kids to meet because the district's current policy is so strict. Perhaps the IT department can come up with a solution. It's also important to check your state's privacy policy. Perhaps student writing should only be posted with a student's first name or a unique screen name. You might also want to consider asking your district to subscribe to SchoolTube, which is a site where students can share their work.

ෆ ◎ ൡ

One of our high school students is doing his senior project on Robert Cormier. He's especially interested in exploring why many of Cormier's novels were often censored. As part of the research, the student is required to use books, periodicals, newspapers, and websites. We have online access to some magazines and newspapers, but they don't date back to when Cormier's works were first challenged. I've done a quick search for online resources, but many of the sites that deal with censorship are blocked in our district. Any suggestions? *April 2013*

There's a book about Cormier's work in the "Authors of Banned Books" series that's called, *Robert Cormier: Banned, Challenged, and Censored* (Enslow, 2008). If you check its chapter notes, you'll find many valuable resources, including the names of websites with their URLs. If your school library doesn't own this series, the local public library may. Consider getting it through interlibrary loan if you can't purchase it by the time the student needs to complete his research. I'm sure that the public library can supply almost anything the student needs—make sure he has a public library card!

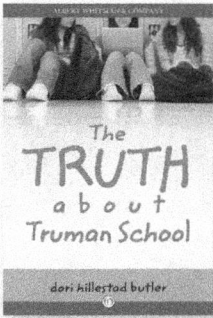

80 ◎ ○8

**Our library's technology manager told me that under the Children's Internet Protection Act (CIPA) we're required to block all social networking sites. Is that true?** *September 2012*

No. CIPA requires libraries that receive E-Rate funding to teach students about cyberbullying and the appropriate use of social networking sites. There are various ways to do that, including offering programs for children and teens or weekend programs aimed at families. Dori Hillestad Butler's *The Truth About Truman School* (Albert Whitman, 2008) is a perfect book to help kids understand the perils of online bullying.

80 ◎ ○8

**Our community has had several unfortunate incidents of students involved in cyberbullying. I'd like to work with our middle schoolers on this issue. Some of our faculty members are supportive of my plans, but others feel that our students' parents are responsible for teaching their kids appropriate online behavior. What's your suggestion?** *January 2011*

This is a hot topic that affects every community, and it's important for students to know how to conduct themselves appropriately on online social networks. I commend you for wanting to work with your students on this issue, and I'm perplexed by the attitude of some of your colleagues. In a perfect world, parents would be totally responsible for teaching their kids how to behave in cyberspace, but unfortunately, that's not the case. There are too many students who don't have parents who are responsible enough to know how to guide them. Plus, adults who should know better have committed some of the worst instances of cyberbullying. Go ahead and develop your curriculum. Then, consider turning it into a parent workshop. I bet the PTA will sponsor the event or your local public library will let you present a community workshop for parents.

$$\wp \; \copyright \; \wp$$

I was surprised to discover that my new school district doesn't have a library policy, especially since we're considering unblocking some social networking sites. I'm especially troubled that there's no Internet-use policy. After meeting with our other librarians, I crafted what I thought was a good policy. But my colleagues balked at it, insisting that they needed more time to think through the issues. If a parent complains about our materials or resources, who's culpable—the district or the librarian? Should I hold my peace or continue to be proactive? *January 2010*
It's sometimes tough to be the new kid on the block. You're absolutely right to be proactive, but all of the stakeholders need to be involved in creating a policy. If there is a district library association, one of its main projects should be to create a library policy. The National School Boards Association's website (www.nsba.org) offers good advice on crafting all sorts of policies. If a parent lodges a complaint, the district is responsible. But don't be surprised if it tries to pass the buck and blame the librarian.

$$\wp \; \copyright \; \wp$$

I heard a speaker say the Supreme Court had ruled that as long as schools and other public entities have CIPA safeguards in place, they can't be sued if a minor accesses an inappropriate website. I'm a high school librarian, and I need help in dealing with a skittish school board. Can you help me? *March 2009*
We live in a litigious society. There's always a risk of being sued, but there are steps that schools can take to reduce the chance of that happening. First, let me explain the provisions of the Children's Internet Protection Act (CIPA). If public schools and libraries receive federal E-Rate discounts or Library Services and Technology grants for Internet service, they're required to use a "technology protection" measure. These measures are not required for institutions that don't receive such funding. This is what CIPA requires:

- ◎ "Technology protection" specifically means that filtering or blocking software must be installed on every computer, including those used by faculty and staff.

◎ The filters must be configured to block visual images that are obscene, harmful to minors, or depict child pornography.

◎ CIPA allows a designated "systems administrator" to disable the filter for an adult who needs information for "bona fide research or other lawful purposes."

◎ The law does not forbid unblocking a site that has been wrongfully blocked, as long as the site does not contain materials defined in the law's criteria for blocking. For example, a site about breast cancer may be unblocked. However, if a picture of a woman's naked breast is shown, even for the purpose of educating girls and women about self-examinations, then unblocking the site may be troublesome. There are those who believe that a woman's bare breast falls under the "obscene" category.

No filter, of course, is foolproof. Some tech-savvy kids can probably figure out a way around it. That's why it's so important for schools to have an Internet acceptable-use policy, which places the responsibility on the user, and lets parents know the school's expectations regarding online use. Students and their parents should sign the policy or agreement, and it should be filed in the media specialist's office. In many ways, this policy offers more protection than CIPA. By the way, it's important to note that some states require all public schools to use filters or risk losing state funding.

Remember: The Children's Internet Protection Act (CIPA) requires schools to use filtering software if they receive E-Rate funds or Institute for Museum and Library Services Act (IMLS) grants. But CIPA applies only to "visual depictions that are obscene, child pornography, or harmful to minors." It makes no reference to text. The courts have recognized that minors have constitutional rights and that filters block constitutionally protected speech. It's imperative that school districts have an Internet Use Policy that addresses student access to online information. The policy should make provisions for unblocking information deemed "educational" upon a student's request. Otherwise, the school district could end up in court.

# 10

## *Issues with Ereaders and Audiobooks*

**Freedom extends beyond format**

New formats and the influx of new devices, as this chapter shows, bring new challenges regarding privacy and access. "There is no difference between sharing books or ereaders and physical books," writes Scales. What matters most is that kids get excited to read. Beyond reading, the audiobook format brings new opportunity for families to share stories together. Regardless of format or device, the ethic remains intact: respect reader privacy. And as for the kids who disrupt the classroom or library by sharing *Fifty Shades of Grey* on an ereader? Scales' advice? Stick to best practices, and focus less on reprisals than on redirection to the classroom tasks at hand. — R. T. M.

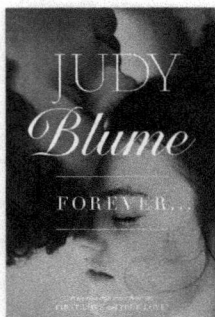

There have been some recent issues with elementary students bringing their ereaders to school and sharing highlighted words and passages from books more appropriate for older readers. The faculty wants to ban all ereaders in school. I think this is a mistake. *November 2014*

There is no difference between sharing books on ereaders and physical books. Every generation of readers has shared books that they felt were "forbidden," whether they were comic books, Judy Blume's *Forever* (Bradbury, 1975), or their mother's copy of *Cosmopolitan*. This is human nature. Banning isn't the answer. I would simply state, "I'm glad you are excited about the book you are reading on your ereader, but we have to focus on school work now. You may share the books with friends after school."

Remember that an adult with a credit card purchases ebooks for a child. Chances are, these adults are celebrating the fact that their child is excited about reading. Faculty should never put themselves in the position of judging what a child is reading.

ཨོ ◎ ଔ

Parents who visit our library's children's room have told me that ereaders have encouraged their kids to read. My son is a struggling reader, and he was very excited when I bought him one. But then we found out that his reading teacher won't allow her students to read ebooks—they can only read books from the school library. How do I handle this? *September 2012*

Rather than focusing on a book's format or where it's shelved, his teacher should concentrate on getting the right title into your son's hands. There's nothing wrong with asking her to explain her rationale. Is she attempting to control her students' reading choices? Let her know that you're willing to experiment with any format that'll help your son. Perhaps she isn't aware that many of the school library's books are also available in digital form, and may be found at the public library. I've heard many censorship cases that deal with the content of library materials, but this is the first I've encountered in which a book's format has been censored. The teacher needs to enter the 21st century. Why not show her some articles about schools that are successfully using iPads and ereaders with their students, such as the September 2012 *School Library Journal* cover story, "Travis's Excellent (Ereader) Adventure"?

**Our midsize public library circulates loads of audiobooks, but lately, many of them have been challenged. When the local paper interviewed our library board chairman, he boldly declared that "children need to be reading, not listening to books." Now the board wants to cut our audiobook budget.** *July 2013*

I'm appalled by his comment. The library board's role is to make policy not value judgments. Many families count on recorded books as a shared activity—ask them to appeal to your library board. Also, make sure that your board knows that the Association of Library Service for Children, a division of the American Library Association, publishes an annual list of "Notable Children's Recordings," which are selected by a committee of professionals from across the country that evaluates new releases for quality, performance, and relevance to children's collections. Public libraries need to purchase these items to stay current with the best in children's recordings.

$\wp \odot \wp$

**A seventh-grade student brought his mother's ereader to class on the last day of school. He passed it around so that students could read passages from** *Fifty Shades of Grey* **(Vintage Books, 2012). It created an uproar and the teacher came to the library to ask my help. I really didn't know what to do.** *September 2013*

This is no different from my generation passing around dog-eared copies of Grace Metalious' *Peyton Place* (Messner, 1956). Don't make a big deal out of the situation. In the future, advise the teacher to simply ask the student to focus on class work and continue reading the book when he gets home.

# 11

# *Curriculum Concerns*

## Book fairs, Common Core, Summer Reading, and more

As several of the selections in this chapter illustrate, book challenges all too often follow the release of annual summer reading lists. In one instance, a parent writes to describe how teachers simply stopped releasing a list, claiming that the inevitable challenges made it not "worth the hassle." Win for the censors! Scales, however, persists in her commitment to turning the tide. In response, she urges a parent to ask for a list for her son, and to then become an anti-censorship advocate by engaging other parents. Other overt censorship efforts cited could keep kids from reading even the like of classics like *To Kill a Mockingbird*. But, Scales notes, most banning efforts backfire and draw more attention to a book than it would have had by languishing on any list: "The irony is that now that the media has reported these incidents, their students are probably having a ball reading these novels," she writes. A silver lining, but just.—R. T. M.

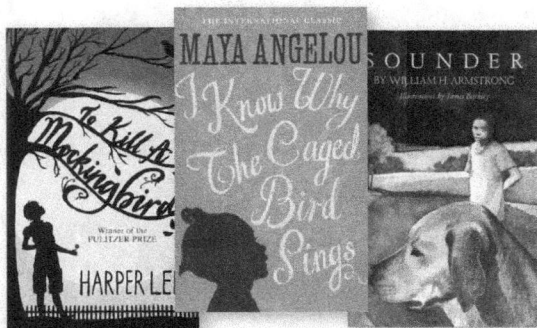

A parent sent a link to the Facts on Fiction website to the school superintendent in my district who directed the English consultant to call a meeting of all English teachers and ask that they not teach any books that are on the site. This leaves out titles such as *To Kill a Mockingbird* (Lippincott, 1960), *I Know Why the Caged Bird Sings* (Random House, 1969), and *Sounder* (Harper and Row, 1969), which they have traditionally taught. The teachers are concerned that they may have very few books to teach. *September 2014*

This site actually uses graphs to rate books for "Mature Content," which includes a detailed graph for Profanity, Sexual Content, Violence/Illegal Activity, Tobacco/Alcohol/Drugs, and Disrespectful/Anti-Social Behavior. The ultra-conservative organization appears to target books typically used in the English or Language Arts curriculum. Take time to peruse the site, and you will quickly see that these "reviewers" don't really know the books, because according to them, *To Kill a Mockingbird* won the Caldecott Medal and the main character is 12. There are no illustrations in *To Kill a Mockingbird*, and the character telling the story is an adult remembering an event that happened when she was six.

Ask teachers to look up every book they teach, and take note of misinformation. Then ask for a meeting with the superintendent. Let him know that teachers know the literature better than the folks at Facts on Fiction, and assure him that they know how to present it to students. This may seem time consuming, but it may be the only way to win this battle. Encourage teachers to ask students to think about the issues that organizations like Facts on Fiction have with books they study. Trust their intelligence to analyze the literature and express their personal opinions, orally and through writing assignments, regarding each work. There will be varying reactions, but literature is intended to make readers think.

৩ ◎ ৫

I'm a middle school librarian and try very hard to work with the faculty. This year I feel challenged, because students from one language arts class tell me that they are allowed to read only nonfiction. I approached the teacher, and he told me that it was because of the Common

**Core State Standards.** *February 2014*

I'm afraid the teacher is misguided. The Common Core State Standards (CCSS) do require attention to nonfiction, but enlightened teachers know that there are exciting ways to use fiction and nonfiction on the same topic. For example, a literary study of *The Book Thief* (Knopf, 2006) also includes opportunities to learn more about the Holocaust by using nonfiction and sites on the Internet. Your best weapon is to thoroughly examine the CCSS. The faculty is likely to listen to you when you show them that you are knowledgeable about the standards.

Find every opportunity to reiterate to students that they may read anything they want outside the curriculum. Perhaps offer a program before and after school that calls their attention to books that might interest them—titles the library has recently acquired or books too good to miss. Students may also enjoy suggesting reads to one another.

There are many different thoughts about summer reading. It makes sense for middle school students to have choices to promote reading. There is also an access issue, unless the school intends to purchase the summer reading choice for every student.

ℰ ◎ ℛ

**Each fall, the government teacher in my high school does a unit to help students distinguish between fact and opinion. He usually has them search five newspapers for articles on one topic and then use different sources to fact check them. This year, the principal told him he couldn't do the unit because some conservative parents had complained about some of the opinions expressed.** *November 2013*

It appears that the principal is more interested in appeasing parents than teaching students. I don't know if your school district has adopted the Common Core State Standards, but these support your case for such instruction. Take a look at English/language arts standards:

> **Reading:** Informational
>
> **Text:** Integration of Knowledge and Ideas RI. 9-10.8 – "Delineate and evaluate the argument and specific claims in a text, assessing whether the reasoning is valid and the evidence is relevant and sufficient; Identify false statements and fallacious reasoning."

This is the best argument I can offer. It's called "Information Literacy," and schools have the responsibility to teach it.

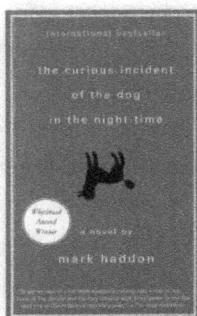

My friend's son (an advanced eighth-grade student in the middle school where I'm a librarian) may take ninth-grade English for credit. The summer reading selection for ninth-graders in the school district is *The Curious Incident of the Dog in the Night-Time* by Mark Haddon (Doubleday, 2003). He is registered for freshman English in the fall, but she doesn't want him to read the novel. I was her easiest target because she doesn't know the English teacher. I didn't know how to handle this. *September 2013*

Do you know for a fact that students weren't given a reading choice? Many school districts allow students to make a summer reading selection from a list of books provided by English teachers. This accommodates various interests and maturity levels. If this isn't the case, then the mother has a choice. She can elect to take her son out of the class and put him in regular eighth-grade English. If she insists that he stay in the class, then he needs to complete the requirement. It sounds as if she will listen to you.

ജ © ര

My son's high school English teachers have stopped recommending books for summer reading. They've had so many challenges to their list, they felt it wasn't worth the hassle. That seems like the coward's way out. *July 2012*

Most people, including teenagers, select books that have been recommended to them by teachers, librarians, or peers. It's too bad that your son's teachers are caving to what's most likely a vocal minority. Ask the teachers to make a list of summer reading recommendations for your son. Better yet, solicit support from parents who think it's important to provide kids with summer reading suggestions—that way, the teachers will hear some positive feedback about their past efforts.

ജ © ര

A high school English teacher asked her students to pick a book on our summer reading list to read. This year, one of her students decided to read a title that wasn't on the list, although another title by the same author was on it. The teacher accepted the student's choice, since it was too late for her to read another book. The problem is that the student's parent has lodged a complaint against the book because it contains some profanity. We have the title in our school library, and I'm worried that we'll soon find ourselves faced with

**a full-blown book challenge. How should I prepare myself?** *January 2012*

First, I think the student and parent should be grateful that the teacher accepted the student's book choice. Not all teachers would be so accommodating. Next, I wouldn't worry about a full-blown challenge until it happens. If the parent complains about the book being in your collection, I'd simply tell her that a library is all about choice. Let her know that the school has many types of readers, and that the school library's mission is to serve all of them. If this doesn't satisfy the parent, then let her go through the proper channels to file a challenge. I have a feeling that she won't have the nerve to do it since it might come to light that that her daughter didn't follow the assignment. Just hold tight.

§© ☼ ©℥

**I've been reading reports that some school administrators have re-moved titles from summer reading lists, including Sherman Alexie's** *The Absolutely True Diary of a Part-Time Indian* **(Little Brown, 2007), Chris Crutcher's** *Angry Management* **(Greenwillow, 2009) and Harper Lee's** *To Kill a Mockingbird* **(Lippincott, 1960). What were these administrators thinking? And how does that mentality affect school library collections?** *September 2011*

These administrators were only thinking about one thing—keeping their noses clean. Most of them don't care about books or reading, and they obviously have no regard for the teachers and librarians who created the lists. The irony is that now that the media has reported these incidents, their students are probably having a ball reading these novels.

It's difficult to determine the effect of censorship on library collections. Some administrators wait for a formal challenge before they remove books from a collection. Others may simply say, "Gone is gone." In the latter case, I hope there's a materials review policy in place so that the librarians can demand that a proper procedure is followed.

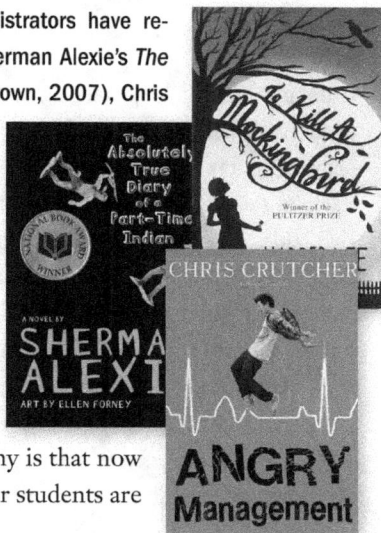

§© ☼ ©℥

**We just passed out information about our public library's summer reading program, and a parent has already complained because it excludes 12-year-olds. She thinks this is a form of censorship. What's your advice?** *July 2011*

I assume that your summer reading program is for elementary school children. I hope that there's a similar program for teens and preteens. My hunch is that even if there's one for teens, that parent isn't ready to turn her 12-year-old over to teen services. Middle-grade kids are sometimes very immature and aren't ready to mingle with 16-year-olds. Libraries should offer some type of summer reading program that allows middle schoolers to participate wherever they feel most comfortable. One option is to ask them to volunteer to help out with younger patrons—that may satisfy some parents. Limiting a summer reading program to a certain age group isn't censorship. But remember, libraries are all about inclusion.

℘ ◎ ◌

**A group of parents is demanding that our school board ban Scholastic Book Clubs in our district's elementary and middle schools. The group isn't objecting to a specific novel—it's objecting to the "junk" offerings. The school board hasn't issued a ruling, but my principal wants to see the book club's latest list of offerings. We need your advice.** *January 2011*

I've had a similar question related to book fairs. The solution is simple. The parents who are causing the ruckus don't have to purchase the materials that they're complaining about. The purpose of these book clubs is to get some sort of reading materials into kids' hands. This means that selections may include award-winning novels as well as high-interest activity books like "Mad Libs." Teachers like using book clubs because they're able to earn free books for their classrooms. And the clubs are a nice alternative for students who live in communities that don't have a bookstore. Please stress to your principal that whether or not one buys books from a book club is a matter of choice. Perhaps the school board already realizes that.

℘ ◎ ◌

**I'm a middle school librarian. For years I've created summer reading lists for our students, and I've never had any problems. But recently a woman who doesn't have a child in our school saw our summer reading list on the school's website and complained about one of the titles—Gail Giles's *Shattering Glass* (Roaring Brook, 2002). I'm worried she'll get some of our parents upset. How should I handle her?** *July 2009*

Tell her that she has a right to her opinion, but that you've created the summer reading list based on students' interests and quality teen literature. My guess is that she belongs to some organized group that's monitoring library collections and services throughout the nation. She would really have no other reason to be looking at your website. Plus, *Shattering Glass* appears on a long list of books that such groups have labeled "inappropriate" for teens. Defend the summer reading list in the same way you'd defend any book in your collection. And be ready to follow your policy if a parent complains.

ഇ ◎ രു

**One of our English teachers plans to teach *A Separate Peace* (Macmillan, 1960) to a class of eighth graders, who will earn high school credit for the course. But there's a problem. A parent who read the novel when she was a high school freshman has complained that the book's language is too graphic for our eighth graders. Should I advise the teacher to change her plans?** *November 2008*
Absolutely not! Instead, the teacher should meet with the parent and explain that the course is for bright eighth-grade students who are taking the class for high school credit. A parent-teacher conference is also a perfect time to have a good book discussion. To spark the conversation, the teacher may want to ask some of the following questions: How did you respond to *A Separate Peace* when you were in ninth grade? How does the story's language define its characters? Gene Forrester, the book's main character, reflects upon his coming-of-age. What does that term mean? How are Gene's emotional conflicts similar to those of most adolescents? How does dealing with these conflicts through a fictional character help adolescents with their own journeys to adulthood?

There's always a chance, of course, that the parent won't change her mind. In that case, the teacher should assure the parent that her child will be offered an alternative book. Since most parents don't want their children singled out in that way, they usually drop their objections.

# 12

# *Difficult Conversations*

## Discussing intellectual freedom with colleagues, library partners, parents, and others

It is clear that often a series of individual conversations are essential opportunities to build a culture of intellectual freedom. But, some of the conversations are very tricky: take the parent who presents to the librarian a list of books her child should not be allowed to read. Or, in another example, the teacher who rejected a book report after it was completed because she didn't like the book it was based on. Or, the school board member who asks the librarian to defend individual books on the fly while she is working with students. Scales' response to each of these instances, and many more here, illustrate the power of brave conversations, rooted in policy and an understanding of the small and large encroachments on intellectual freedoms. Why brave? Because all too often issues arise from people who carry authority. The librarian's role is clear, indicates Scales: educate, educate, educate.—*R. T. M*

Last year my school held a book fair at a local bookstore. It was a very successful event, because parents bought books for all ages, including adult books. One member of the PTA board wasn't happy, as she felt students perused books that weren't appropriate for them. Now our principal is reluctant about holding such an event this year. *November 2014*

When I was a middle school librarian, I held some in-store book fairs around holiday time. They were always a big hit because adults were buying gifts for all ages, and the proceeds from the book fair helped fund library programs. I never worried about students looking at books that some adults may have deemed "inappropriate." The students who attended the in-store event came with their parents. It was up to the adults to steer their readers to areas of the bookstore they preferred for them to shop. I did station myself in the young readers section so that I could tell students about titles I thought they would enjoy.

Ask your principal: How is an in-store book fair different from a parent taking their child to a bookstore? There is no difference, except that you are there to tell readers about books that a bookstore clerk may know nothing about. Don't allow one voice of the PTA board to sunset a successful event for the school.

ฌ ◎ ଔ

My library works with a local juvenile detention center to provide materials for incarcerated teens ages 13 and up. I'm a teen librarian assigned to this initiative. The juvenile detention officers often question the fiction I bring. They don't want me bringing any books dealing with drugs and alcohol, sex, street violence, bullying, etc. Their rationale is that these types of books send the wrong message to teens already in trouble. *June 2014*

Incarcerated youth didn't get there by reading books. These youth should expect access to a wide range of books and materials that interest them, and that includes fiction. You may have to convince the officers by showing them how teens think and respond. This can be done through a "book club" approach, where teens read and talk about books they have read. Use open-ended questions that explore conflict in the novel, and talk about the resolution. For example, I suspect that most incarcerated teens would gravitate toward Sherman Alexie's *The Absolutely True Diary of a Part-Time Indian* (Little Brown, 2007), Walter Dean Myers's *Monster* (Harper-Collins, 1999), and Jay Asher's *Thirteen Reasons Why* (Penguin, 2007). These books may actually get teens talking about issues in ways that a counselor or arbitrator may never accomplish. Remind the officers that these incarcerated teens have First Amendment rights, and that includes the freedom to read (see addendum "Prisoners Right to Read: An Interpretation of the Library Bill of Rights," p. 134).

ॐ ◎ ◯

A fifth-grade language arts teacher in my school told her students that they weren't allowed to read a book that wasn't in our elementary school library. I've had several parents call and complain to me. I asked the teacher why she would make such a demand, and she said that several students turned in book reports on dystopian novels and she didn't think such books were age-appropriate. What should I do? *November 2013*

Turn to the policy manual of your school district. I doubt it restricts students to materials in the school library. This teacher is clearly allowing her personal beliefs to abridge the rights of kids to choose books that interest them. If she is so concerned about what they are reading for book reports, then she needs to make the assignment more specific. Instead of telling them what they may not read, she should suggest certain titles or genres from which to choose. Then, do the students a favor and lead them to dystopian novels in the school library collection. They may enjoy the books more if they don't have to write book reports on them.

ॐ ◎ ◯

Another elementary school in my district had several challenges last year. Since my school library has a number of parent volunteers, I thought it wise to provide them training in hopes of avoiding challenges in my school. What should I tell them? *September 2013*

Two main points:

◎ Student privacy is a requirement

◎ Leave reader guidance to you.

I personally recommend that parent volunteers be used for more clerical types of jobs. If parents want to read aloud to students, then make the reading choice to-gether. Never ask a parent to read aloud something they aren't comfortable reading.

**Students in a sophomore English class in my school were asked to write an original short story. One student used a lot of profanity in his. The teacher thinks the language is inappropriate and is afraid that she may get in trouble with the principal. She wants to fail the student. I told her that would be a mistake. What should we do?** *July 2013*

If she didn't specify that students weren't allowed to use profanity in their stories, then she doesn't have ground to stand on. Please advise the teacher to judge and grade the story on its merit, and not on issues of language. Are the stories for publication, a contest, to be read aloud in class? If not, then why is she afraid that the principal will question the assignment? She will create a larger problem if she reprimands the student.

ഇ ◎ ര

**As I was preparing a library card for a new student, she handed me a two-page list of books that her mother won't allow her to read. Then later on, her mother called and told me she expected me to monitor what her daughter was reading. What should I do?** *January 2013*

You need to tell the mother that it's not your role to monitor students' reading. If she has an issue with the titles that her daughter chooses, then she needs to take it up with her. Also, make sure the mother understands that you have students whose parents want them to read the books on her list. My bet is that the girl will find a way to get her hands on those titles without her mother's knowledge. Any book that is "forbidden" is more enticing to young readers.

ഇ ◎ ര

**A sixth-grade teacher asked his students to select a book of their choice to share with the class. When a student picked a book about evolution, he made her return it and then asked me to justify why I had books on evolution in our library. The girl was upset because she was genuinely interested in the subject, and I felt as though my professional judgment was being challenged. How should I handle this?** *November 2013*

You should talk to the student first because the teacher has probably thoroughly humiliated her. Let her know that there's nothing wrong with reading about evolution, and perhaps she should talk to her teacher about the assignment. After all, he gave his class permission to choose any book that interested them and he can't take that back just because he doesn't agree with a student's selection. Make sure that the student knows that she can borrow books about evolution anytime she wants.

I'd also request a conference with the teacher. It's time that he understands that library materials represent many different ideas, beliefs, and theories. He also needs to understand that a library provides materials to satisfy students' individual interests. In this case, the student is interested in evolution.

ဢ ◎ ಜ

**A father called me to complain after a parent volunteer told his son he shouldn't be reading books about witchcraft. What should I do? The volunteer helps me three days a week, and I really need her help.** *November 2011*
You may really need her help, but you need to inform her that she shouldn't judge children's reading choices. Tell her that we all have different beliefs, and that libraries recognize and celebrate these differences. If the volunteer gets angry and quits, then it's the students' gain. I suggest that you plan volunteer training that covers this topic. You can save yourself a lot of grief in the future.

ဢ ◎ ಜ

**Every month, teachers from the YMCA check out 50 books from our library to use in their early childcare program. Two of their parents have filed formal complaints about our Mother Goose books because they think they're too violent. Now, our director is wondering whether it's worth serving the Y's program since we've gotten so many complaints. Those of us in children's services would hate to drop the program.** *July 2011*
First, congratulations for offering such a wonderful service to your local YMCA. What a model outreach program! Handle the challenge to the Mother Goose books the same way you'd handle any other challenge. Allow the complaints to go through the complete process. I'm certain those books will be retained.

Two challenges don't sound like a lot, and I'd think that your library director would be more concerned about serving your community than avoiding parents' complaints. Ask the YMCA's childcare director if they have a book selection policy for their teachers to use. I bet they don't. Offer to help them develop one that supports their program and the community they serve. I bet they'll welcome your guidance. Finally, offer to conduct workshops that'll show parents how to use all types of books with preschoolers, including Mother Goose books.

ဢ ◎ ಜ

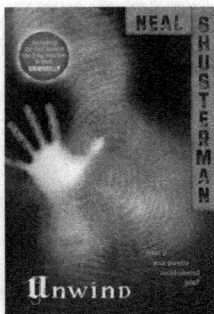

I'm a librarian at a K-5 school. A parent complained that her son's fourth-grade teacher recommended that he read Neal Shusterman's *Unwind* (Simon & Schuster, 2007). The parent said that her son is a "gifted" reader, but he's very immature. She decided to read the book and was horrified that a teacher would recommend it to a fourth grader. We don't have the book in our library collection. She borrowed it from the public library's teen section. Now the teacher wants me to defend her on the grounds that she was recommending books on a "higher reading level." *July 2011*

At the risk of sounding flip, I'd suggest telling the teacher, "You're in this one alone." *Unwind* is a fabulous book. It's a gripping, thought-provoking thriller. But it isn't for fourth graders, regardless of how gifted they are. I seriously doubt that the teacher has read it. I'm curious about why she recommended that title. Did someone tell her about it? Did she read a review of it? Let the teacher and the parent know that libraries are filled with books for "gifted" nine-year-olds that'll challenge them to think about complex issues—books like Madeleine L'Engle's *A Wrinkle in Time* (Farrar, Straus, and Giroux, 1962), Ellen Raskin's *The Westing Game* (Dutton, 1978) and Norton Juster's *The Phantom Tollbooth* (Random House, 1961) to name just a few. Encourage the teacher to check with you before she recommends a book to her students, especially if it isn't in your collection and it's in the public library's teen collection.

∞ ◎ ∞

I'm the children's services manager for a public library system. I just had an irate parent complain about an employee who wouldn't let her 11-year-old son take out *Chains* (Simon & Schuster, 2008) by Laurie Halse Anderson. The employee defended herself by saying that the book is classified as YA. This has become a big issue for our library system, especially in our six branches, where most of the employees aren't trained professionals. Do you have any suggestions? *May 2011*

Start by training your employees who aren't librarians but are doing the work of professionals. They need to learn how to deal with the public, proper reading-guidance skills, and the fine line between children's and young adult books. You didn't tell me how old children must be before they're allowed

free access to your YA collection. Perhaps your library needs to offer some type of "parent approved" card that lets kids access your entire collection. I'm sure there are parents who would welcome that. By the way, why isn't *Chains* in both your children's and YA collections? There are many 11-year-olds who can handle it. Yes, I'm aware that the book contains violent content, but it's set during the American Revolutionary War. You can't have a book about war without violence. Be honest and think about whom you're protecting by putting the book only in the YA section. Is it the children or the library? Here lies an ethical issue that librarians face on a daily basis.

ഇ ◎ ൠ

**My seventh-grade son did a project on the works of the Old Masters and downloaded images of their art for his PowerPoint presentation. Although the teacher had approved the project, she stopped him in the middle of his presentation and told him he couldn't continue to show his slides because they included nude images. My son was very upset. What should I do?** *August 2010*

I would definitely have a conversation with the teacher. I'm not sure how a student can be expected to give a presentation on the art of the Old Masters without displaying any images. I think that you should remind her that your son completed the assignment on a topic that she'd approved. I'm quite certain that she'll tell you the nude images would have disrupted the class. Be prepared to tell her that students need to be taught not to laugh at art, but, instead, to embrace it. How else will they learn the power and the value of art if they aren't exposed to it in school? You might also suggest that the teacher visit the school library's art section. I just bet there are books about the Old Masters that include nudes. Your son's classmates have probably found them—now that their teacher has fueled their curiosity.

ഇ ◎ ൠ

**My ninth-grade daughter loves Stephenie Meyer's "Twilight" series (Little, Brown). But recently a friend's mother lectured her about how "bad" those books are. My daughter didn't know what to say and came home in tears, because she was embarrassed in front of a friend. She doesn't want me to call the mother. What should I do?** *September 2010*

No adolescent wants to be embarrassed, so I wouldn't make matters worse by calling the mother. Instead, you should have a discussion with your daughter about her rights as a reader, and give her some clear talking points. That way, she'll be prepared the next time someone challenges her reading choices. There's probably another very embarrassed person in this scenario: your daughter's friend. I bet she wants to read the "Twilight" books. Why don't you invite her over for a slumber party?

৪১ ◎ ৫১

At my suggestion, my eighth-grade son wrote a book report on Robert Cormier's *The Chocolate War* (Pantheon, 1974). His teacher returned the report ungraded and told him that she didn't approve of his choice and he needed to read something else. My problem with this situation is that she didn't tell her students in advance that she had to approve their choices. I try to stay out of things like this (I'm an English teacher at another school), but this time, I felt I should speak up. When I called the teacher, she didn't back down. My son didn't want me to go to the principal, so I didn't. I'm curious to know what you think. *September 2010*

I'm on your son's side 100 percent, and I'm glad you called the teacher. It's difficult to understand how a teacher could refuse to grade a book report based on a personal dislike of a book. I bet she wouldn't like a number of books that her students write about if she were familiar with their content. She just happened to know *The Chocolate War* or its reputation as a banned book. I understand that your son didn't want you to make more trouble for him by going to the principal, but someone needs to let this teacher know that she can't wait until after a book report has been submitted to approve or disapprove of the book. Also, I can't help but wonder what would happen if you, or another parent, disapproved of a book that she had chosen to teach. I hope that somewhere along the way she learns to respect her students' choices as much as she wants them to respect hers.

৪১ ◎ ৫১

One of our teachers, who requires her fourth graders to read at least five Newbery Medal books, wondered why the library doesn't have every single Newbery winner. I've tried to explain that some of them are too mature for elementary school students, but she thinks I'm practicing censorship—and she's garnering support from other faculty members. What should I do? *September 2009*

I agree that there are a few Newbery-winning books that are too mature for some fourth graders. The Newbery rules state that books intended for children from "birth to 14" are eligible for the award. This broad age range is troubling to some librarians and teachers. For example, some educators feel that Katherine Patterson's *Jacob Have I Loved* (Crowell, 1980) and Lois Lowry's *The Giver* (Houghton 1993) are more appropriate for children ages 12 to 14. But fourth graders have a wide range of abilities and maturity levels and should have access to those books. Your job is to provide books that meet the needs of all of the school's students. Although the teacher's charge may be unfounded, this is a good time for you to examine your book-selection process. How do you decide which titles are too mature for students? Is your decision based on reviews? Have you read all of the Newbery winners? Has the teacher read all of them? Have you suggested that she also include Newbery Honor books? The silver seal means quality, too. And this gives children more reading choices.

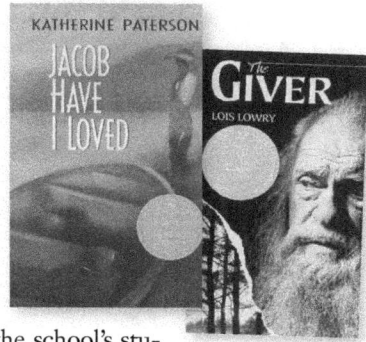

In the spirit of team building I suggest that you form a faculty book club. Begin by having the group read all of the Newbery Medal and Honor books. Discuss each title's literary merits as well as its potential child appeal. You might even invite students to offer their views. Anytime you can turn "negative" opinions into a positive outcome, it makes everyone a winner—especially young readers.

ဆ ◎ ⚬

**Our town has had a few problems at the local shopping mall with gang-related crimes, which have sparked daily letters to the newspaper. One writer wants all books that deal with gangs removed from our public and school libraries. The public library has refused to go along with that scheme, but it looks like our school superintendent agrees with it. How should my fellow school librarians and I respond to him?** *May 2009*

Respond in the same way you would with any book challenge. Gather supportive reviews, statements, etc., and remind the superintendent of your selection policies. Let the superintendent and school board know that reading books about gangs may help students express their fears. What most adults, including some superintendents, don't realize is that the real danger is in not talking about it. Remember that many parents aren't equipped to discuss "tough topics" with their kids. Maybe they need the guidance of a good school librarian. The names of recommended books about gangs as well as discussion questions for students could be posted on your school's website. Maybe if you suggest that idea to the superintendent, he'll change his mind.

$\wp \ \textcircled{\tiny{©}} \ \wp$

**An irate parent recently stormed into our school and complained that members of a religious group were standing outside our gate, handing out copies of the New Testament to students. Our secretary made things worse by getting into a verbal battle with the parent. Can you offer any advice?** *November 2008*

Since the group wasn't standing on school property, it probably wasn't breaking the law. However, some communities have local ordinances that prohibit "religious or any special interest groups" from distributing literature within a specified distance of school property. If your community has such an ordinance, the school should notify the local police. My bet is that the religious group knows the law, and it was walking the "straight and narrow." Regardless, parents should be encouraged to talk to their children about whether it's appropriate to accept the books. Most schools have a parent newsletter and website to help get the word out. But be sure to present the information in an unbiased way. In other words, stick to the facts. I'd also encourage your school to turn this into a teachable moment by talking to students about their First Amendment rights and letting them know that they have the right to accept or reject the literature. Finally, make sure your school secretary understands that she was out of line. She should refer upset parents directly to your administrators.

$\wp \ \textcircled{\tiny{©}} \ \wp$

**Every year, the PTA sponsors a book fair at our middle school. Lately they haven't been pleased with the selections they've received from the book-fair company. Although I'm the school librarian, I'm never included in the selection process. But when the books arrive, the PTA insists that I identify the titles that could cause trouble in the community. I feel like I'm being asked to be a censor. What should I do?** *July 2008*

Unfortunately, this is an all too familiar story. Since many PTA members aren't familiar with most middle school titles, they usually opt to take the book-fair company's preselected package rather than making their own selections from the company's catalog—and that's never a good idea. If the PTA is asking you to identify potentially troublesome titles, they are indeed asking you to be a censor.

What can you do? I'd recommend that you arrange a conference with the PTA's board; explain that you know the books and your students' reading interests, and you'd like the opportunity to select titles for the book fair. This puts you in the role of a book selector, rather than a book censor. Also, request that the book fair become a regular part of your library's program.

Once you've developed a partnership with the PTA, I'd suggest that you interview various book-fair companies to see which one best suits your school's needs. Some questions that you might ask include: How does your company select its titles? Do you accept special requests for titles that aren't in your catalog? Do all of the books come without reading-level stickers or other prejudicial labels? Will our school only receive the titles we've ordered? It's important to inquire about a company's selection practices. That way you can avoid those that "pre-censor" books by not offering certain titles to your school.

80 ◎ ଓ

**Just when I thought** *The Chocolate War* **(Pantheon, 1974) was finally safe, a group of parents is trying to remove it from my son's middle school library. My son tells me that all of his friends are reading the books' "objectionable" passages and laughing at them. What should I tell him?** *July 2008*

Every generation has a book or several books that get passed around the classroom with marked passages. There's something about the "forbidden" that causes readers to take notice. I would make this a teachable moment and explain the importance of reading the entire novel. You might even invite your son's friends to a book discussion about *The Chocolate War*. Ask them if their view of the "objectionable" passages changes by the end of the novel. Explain to them that taking passages or words out of context is a tactic that censors often use. You might even relate specific examples like the "mating scene" in *A Day No Pigs Would Die* (Knopf, 1972) by Robert Newton Peck. If they read that novel, they'll see why this scene is essential to the story.

80 ◎ ଓ

**A friend asked me to recommend a book for her 11-year-old daughter. When I suggested Olive's** *Ocean* **(Greenwillow, 2003), she told me she didn't want her daughter to read it because the novel was challenged for its sexually explicit content and offensive language.**

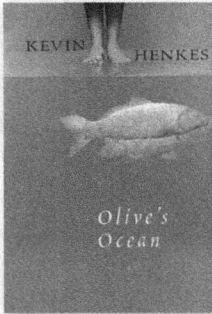

I immediately recommended something else, but later on, I was angry at myself for not explaining the perils of censorship to her. *July 2008*

You chose a book that's popular with many 11-year-old girls. You did the right thing by offering another recommendation, but I would find a convenient time to discuss this matter with your friend. The issue goes beyond just this one title. Your friend needs to understand the danger of labeling a book "offensive" without reading it. You might also explain that her daughter will likely read the book because others are reading it. The best approach that your friend can take is to read the book and discuss it with her daughter. She may not listen to you, but at least you tried to explain. There's always the chance that she will love the book. The censorship war has to be fought one battle at a time. Sometimes we win, and sometimes we lose. But we can never win if we don't fight.

℘ ◎ ℭ

The recent controversy over Philip Pullman's *The Golden Compass* (Knopf) has caused some of our middle school parents to call me. They aren't asking me to remove the book; they simply want to know if they should allow their children to see the film version. *January 2008*

Since the movie has been long available this may be a moot point. But I want to address this question because parents often ask librarians to judge the merits of books, movies, and other products for young people. It's our role to serve our young users and their parents, but it isn't our role to "be" the parent. The best way to answer such a request is to simply say, "I can't make that decision for you. I can tell you that readers of fantasy love Pullman's books."

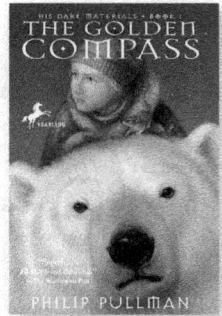

℘ ◎ ℭ

A parent recently asked me why some of our books contain language that's inappropriate for students to use in school. What should I tell her? *January 2007*

Explain to her that a library offers books about a variety of characters that may live in vastly different environments. Plus, just because you've included a title in your collection, doesn't mean that you're endorsing its language or ideas. It's also not unusual to have students who will point out a novel's "offensive language" and then alert their parents. If that happens, turn the experience into a teachable moment by showing the student how to do a thorough literary analysis: What is the essential conflict? Who is the main character? How does the author use language to define that character? Appealing to a student's intellect will often diffuse a potential problem with a parent. Now is also a good time for you to become reacquainted with your school's collection-development policy. Make sure it includes a statement about controversial books and materials.

ഇ © ശ

**Last year, our school board decided to allow some of our eighth graders to take a high school English course for credit. Although these 13-year-olds are eager to take the course, many of their parents feel that the literature is too mature for them. Should we revise the curriculum to accommodate their parents?** *May 2007*
When it comes to maturity, there's often not much difference between eighth and ninth graders. Since this particular course carries high school credit, its content is probably the same as a regular ninth-grade English class. Parents who are concerned about the maturity level of the literature in freshman English may elect to have their children wait another year before taking the course. By the way, every school should offer its gifted middle school students a challenging curriculum—without expecting them to begin accruing high school credits. That approach gives educators more flexibility in selecting literature. If parents are assured that gifted students are intellectually challenged, then they'll be more likely to be satisfied that the school is properly serving the needs of their children.

ഇ © ശ

**One of our school board members frequently browses our library's shelves and often asks me to justify the titles in our collection. He typically interrupts me when I'm working with students. In fact, it's gotten to the point where I feel he's harassing me. What should I do?** *July 2007*
It's possible that your district has a board policy about visitors during the school day. This policy should include unannounced visits from a school board member. Tell the board member that you're happy to speak with him, but that a more appropriate

time to talk would be when school isn't in session. Also, let him know that students are your first priority. You might even suggest a specific time and day for him to drop by. That puts the ball in your court and says you aren't intimidated by him. When you do meet, give him a copy of the materials selection policy. Discuss your policy with him and make sure he understands the library's mission. My bet is that this will satisfy him. If not, seek help from your principal or superintendent.

ഇ ◎ ര

**A parent of a second grader was upset by the bad grammar used in Barbara Parks' "Junie B. Jones" series. What should I tell her?** *September 2007*

The "Junie B. Jones" series is easy to read and extremely funny—no wonder emerging readers love it. Explain to the parent that the dialogue simply reflects the age of the main character. Most five- and six-year-olds haven't mastered the rules of grammar—and neither has Junie B. You might encourage the parent and child to read aloud together one of the books. Then, suggest that the parent read aloud the same story, this time using proper grammar in place of the offending phrases: How do those changes affect the book's tone and humor? That's a great way for parents and children to see how language and dialogue are used in literature. Maybe that activity will help the parent see Junie B. through the eyes of a young reader.

ഇ ◎ ര

**Our public library has a large graphic novel collection. But lately, some of our staff have complained that many of the graphic novels are demeaning to women. How do I deal with that?** *September 2007*

Remind them that graphic novels are selected using the same standards that apply to other library materials. Also remind them that before you order them, you consult reviews in established review resources, such as *School Library Journal* and *Booklist*.

Of course, some graphic novels are serials; so libraries may subscribe to them just as they do magazines. Just because a patron or staff member is offended by a particular article or ad in a specific issue of a magazine, that doesn't mean the library should cancel its subscription. I grew up reading Archie comic books, featuring Veronica and Betty, who were portrayed as being large busted and flirtatious. But I never saw this as demeaning. I simply looked forward to the next issue.

The comic books of my youth have given birth to today's graphic novels, which have become a serious art form. In fact, one of them, Gene Luen Yang's *American Born Chinese* (First Second, 2006), was a 2006 National Book Award Finalist and the winner of the 2007 Printz Award, honoring excellence in young adult literature. Young readers have embraced graphic novels—it's time for librarians to do the same. [Editor's note: ALA has since added further support for the value of graphic novels via the relatively new Will Eisner Graphic Novel Grant program.]

જી ◎ ભ

**We've observed Banned Books Week for years, but our new principal wants us to discontinue the practice. She doesn't feel that Banned Book activities are curriculum based and fears they may actually lead to more challenges. How can I help her see the importance of this special week?** *September 2007*

Many school administrators need to be convinced that Banned Books Week is important. Let your principal know that the purpose of the observance is to make Americans aware of their First Amendment rights. You'll also want to explain that although the titles featured in the American Library Association's Banned Books Week materials have been challenged, most of them have never been banned. That's largely due to the efforts of librarians, booksellers, and the national sponsors of Banned Books Week, who have defended our freedom to read. Every school in our nation teaches its students about the United States Constitution—so Banned Books Week is applicable to your curriculum. Ask a social studies and language arts teacher to help you develop Banned Books Week activities. That type of teamwork may help change your principal's mind.

જી ◎ ભ

**Our faculty doesn't understand the differences among a censored book, a banned book, and a challenged book. Can you please give me a simple explanation to share with them?** *September 2007*

A book is censored when someone alters or blacks out its words or visual images because they disapprove of the message. For example, in some instances, markers have been used to "clothe" nude images in library art books. Those are blatant acts of censorship. A banned book is one that has been removed from a library or class-room because an individual or committee doesn't think that patrons should have access to it. A challenged book is one whose content has been questioned. Schools and libraries should have a policy that deals with challenged materials. In most cases, these titles remain in the library until the challenge has been resolved.

ఴ ◎ ౬

**Our English teachers don't want us to circulate the novels that they teach. The reason? They'd rather not have their students reading the books ahead of time. What should I tell them?** *September 2007*

This is such an old argument. First, let them know that the purpose of a school library is to provide students open access to age-appropriate materials. My advice? Tell the teachers it never hurts for students to read a book more than once. After all, a teacher's job is to help kids notice things they wouldn't have noticed on their own. A good example is Lois Lowry's *The Giver* (Houghton Mifflin, 1993), a popular novel that's often taught in middle school. I've had sixth graders read the book solely for its story line. Then, the following year, when they studied it in seventh grade, they were able to grasp its complex themes a little better. Novels that are taught in school should always be multilayered—that way, students are guaranteed a deeper reading experience even if they've already read the book.

ఴ ◎ ౬

**A parent complained that *July's People* (Viking, 1981) by Nadine Gordimer wasn't appropriate for his 10th-grade son. Our principal told him that it was required reading—and his son had to read it or else he would fail global studies. How can we avoid another situa-tion like that?** *September 2006*

Though schools do have freedom in designing curriculum, it's always a good idea to offer students a reading alternative. If your district doesn't have a policy that addresses this issue, speak with your principal, curriculum supervisors, or super-intendent and encourage them to propose such a policy. In the end, it protects the teacher, curriculum, and school from a potentially volatile situation.

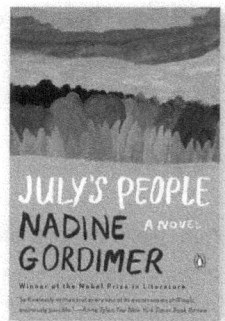

Librarians often have to deal with censorship cases. I recommend that they meet with teachers at the beginning of the school year and suggest that their colleagues select an alternative novel for each unit. It should be one that follows the objectives of the class, and in no way jeopardizes the integrity of the curriculum. Most students will never request another title, but allowing a choice removes the likelihood of a challenge that affects all of the students.

℘ ◎ ℃

**A teacher told a gifted fourth-grade student that she couldn't read** *Are You There God? It's Me, Margaret* **(Bradbury, 1970) because it has a third-grade reading level. What should I tell the teacher?**
*September 2006*

Blume's novel mirrors the life of a fourth or fifth grader. This is an unfortunate situation: the student is being restricted because of the book's reading level, and she's being punished because she is gifted (which, of course, doesn't mean that she is more mature). If she reads the novel, she may discover that it's a quick read and the vocabulary is not very challenging for her. On the other hand, she'll discover a protagonist with whom she can identify—someone who is dealing with the joys and pains of growing up. Explain to the teacher that sometimes students just want to read for the pure fun of it—and because they need a story's main character to be their friend. The purpose of the library is to provide all types of materials for students and to allow them to read freely. That may be a good topic for a future in-service program or faculty meeting.

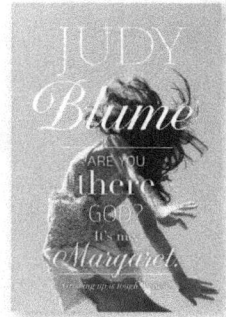

# 13

## *Object Lessons*

### More advice on confronting censorship

"I live in fear that someone will challenge one of our books." That from a librarian who feels unprepared by library school and unsupported in her work setting. This uncomfortable reality is not something to just accept, notes Scales. As she does throughout her columns Scales speaks professional to professional: charging the librarians and educators alike to step up to the great responsibility at hand. She supplies resources, inspiration, reality checks, and a sense of urgency. She sets the expectation for continuous effort, even in the face of fear. "Don't be frightened," she writes. "Just get prepared."—*R. T. M.*

**What's the difference between banning a book and having one removed from a collection after it has been reevaluated?** *January 2007*

When books are banned from a library's collection, they're removed without due process—and without sound reason. That's one of the reasons why the American Library Association recommends that every school district create its own collection development policy—one that includes selection criteria as well as procedures for dealing with formal book challenges. Most districts have reconsideration committees, made up of teachers, librarians, administrators, community members, and students. When its members evaluate a challenged title, they should carefully consider their school or district's collection development policy. That way, the reevaluation process will be as objective as possible. If a committee decides that a title isn't appropriate, then it must be removed from a library's shelves.

ഇ ◎ ଔ

**When I was in high school, I don't remember anyone ever challenging the books we read in English class. Why has there been a sudden increase in the number of challenges? And what do I tell our English teachers who've become "gun-shy" about selecting books for their classes?** *May 2008*

I don't think there's been a sudden surge of book challenges. I think we're just doing a better job of keeping track of them. The American Library Association's Office for Intellectual Freedom (www.ala.org/ala/oif), the National Coalition Against Censorship (www.ncac.org), and the National Council of Teachers of English (www.ncte.org) each maintains a database of books that have been challenged or banned in schools and libraries. These resources are important sources of information and advice for those of us who are battling book challenges in our schools. Maya Angelou's *I Know Why the Caged Bird Sings*, Harper Lee's *To Kill a Mockingbird*

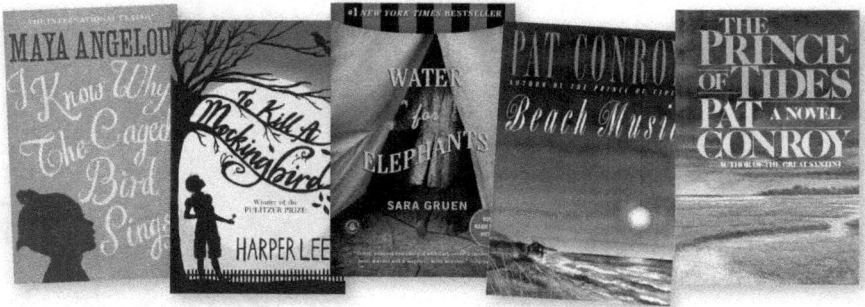

(Lippincott, 1960), and Sara Gruen's *Water for Elephants* have recently been challenged in schools. And there's also a very tough battle being fought in West Virginia over two of Pat Conroy's books—*Beach Music* and *The Prince of Tides*. Conroy's novels, which were used in an elective AP English class, were banned because of their depictions of dysfunctional families and violent acts and their use of obscene language. The author has joined local students and teachers in asking the school board to reverse its decision.

It's difficult to be brave when your book selections are being scrutinized by community members, but English teachers must not let these challenges discourage them from using quality books in the classroom. I'd encourage your teachers to visit NCTE's website, which offers guidance in creating their own criteria for book selections. Ultimately, school-board-approved criteria are the best defense in dealing with book challenges.

80 ◎ ⋊

I have seen a recent push by the American Library Association (ALA) Office for Intellectual Freedom (OIF) to report any challenge to library materials. I've been afraid to let ALA know when there has been a challenge in my library. Why is reporting so important? *July 2013*
Don't be afraid. The ALA OIF is there to help you. The information that is reported is kept confidential unless the person filing the complaint wishes for it to go public. ALA uses the data to help guide other libraries in the nation with similar cases. In addition, the data is used in determining the most challenged materials in a given year. It is especially helpful when the office knows the resolution to a case.

80 ◎ ⋊

Our state library association has sponsored a children's book award for the past 35 years. Students in grades three through five are asked to read five books from a list of 20 that have been selected by a statewide committee of 15 teachers and librarians. Then, in the spring, students vote for their favorite titles. Over the years, we've had an occasional challenge to some of the books on the list. But this year, a librarian on the committee didn't like one of the books the group chose. She demanded that the book be removed from the list or she would go to the press and tell them it wasn't an appropriate title for children to read. She ended up turning the selection process into a fiasco. I'm chairing next year's

**committee. What should I do if this happens again?** *September 2010*

I wish I knew the name of that book, but in the grand scheme of things, it doesn't really matter. On the other hand, if the selection committee allowed itself to be bullied by one of its members, that does matter. I suggest that you begin planning how you're going to lead your committee next year. The first time it meets, make sure to discuss the following points: What does it mean to be a good committee member and a good listener? How will your group create its reading list and craft the final list of books? What's an appropriate way of dealing with controversial titles? And finally, how will you sell the list? As chair, your job is to keep your committee focused and on track. When a committee has a good leader, its members are proud to be part of the process. If one of your colleagues tries to derail the selection process, you may need to have a private conversation with that person about the importance of working together as a group.

ℬ ◎ ℭ

**I'm in library school and one of our assignments is to chart the challenges to the "Harry Potter" series. I've noticed in the literature that new challenges arose every time a new "Harry Potter" book was published. Is that typical when the first book in a series has been challenged?** *November 2011*

Yes, that's what typically happens. After the first book in Dav Pilkey's "Captain Underpants" series (Scholastic) was challenged, each new title faced challenges for identical reasons: "unruly behavior," "language," and "underwear." *The Agony of Alice* (Atheneum, 1985), the first volume in Phyllis Reynolds Naylor's "Alice" series, wasn't challenged until the later titles triggered concerns because of "references to alcohol" and "questions about sex and sexuality." *Anastasia Krupnik* (Houghton Mifflin, 1979), the first book in Lois Lowry's "Anastasia" series, was challenged for its "language," which sparked additional complaints about the series' subsequent titles. And Suzanne Collins's entire "Hunger Games" trilogy (Scholastic) has been challenged for its "violence" and "dystopian society."

Sometimes a body of unrelated work by a particular writer ends up being challenged. This has certainly been the case for books by Judy Blume, Laurie Halse Anderson, Ellen Hopkins, Walter Dean Myers, Robert Lipsyte, Chris Lynch, and Chris Crutcher.

ℬ ◎ ℭ

**One of our community members wants all of the titles on the American Library Association's "100 Most Frequently Challenged Books" list removed from our school district's libraries. How should I handle this?** *March 2007*

Tell him that you're happy that he has the list, and you're looking forward to talking to him about the books after he has read them. Remind him that each title must be formally challenged before a hearing can occur. There's a good chance he'll never make a formal challenge.

ΩÖ◎Ω

**I work in the children's room at a large metropolitan public library. A teenage girl was sitting at one of our tables when her cell phone rang. The ring tone was a song that has a string of four-letter words, including the "F" word. I'd never heard anything like it, and I didn't know how to handle the situation. My tendency was to ask, "Does your mother know about that ringtone?" What should I have done?** *July 2011*

Simple! You should have gone over and said, "Cell phones must be silenced in the public library."

ΩÖ◎Ω

**I live in fear that someone will challenge one of our books. I'm not very confident about dealing with censorship because I didn't have a single course about it in library school. Now that I'm an elementary school librarian, I feel that my library school failed me. Where can I go for help?** *July 2009*

I don't know very many library schools that offer a course that deals exclusively with intellectual freedom issues. Most deal with this topic in collection development and administration courses. I'm puzzled that you didn't have a single course that dealt with censorship. Intellectual freedom is the heart of library service. Many colleges and universities offer online courses that will prepare you for dealing with challenges.

There are also online seminars offered through the American Library Association (ALA). Plus, there are a vast number of articles that deal with materials selection and policies. ALA offers an Intellectual Freedom Manual, and its Office for Intellectual Freedom has helpful information and guidelines on its website. (See the Appendices.)

You must take the responsibility to prepare yourself. Check your school district Board Policy Manual to see if there are materials selection policies. If not, find out the appropriate person to talk to about getting those policies written. Without selection and materials review policies, you and your district's librarians are quite vulnerable should a challenge arise. Don't be frightened. Just get prepared.

ဏ ◎ ଔ

**A sixth-grade teacher at my affluent private school wants to teach** *The Watsons Go to Birmingham—1963* **(Delacorte, 1995) by Christopher Paul Curtis. But a parent, an African-American lawyer, objects because she doesn't want her daughter to know that the Civil Rights Movement took place. How can I help?** *November 2006*

All teachers should have complete freedom to select novels for classroom study as long as they adhere to school guidelines. I suggest arranging a meeting between the parent and teacher so he can explain his lesson plan and why he chose the novel.

Ask the parent to offer her legal expertise by making a presentation to the class about the Civil Rights Act of 1964. This type of parental involvement usually turns a complaint into something more constructive. If this doesn't work, offer the student an alternative novel while her classmates complete their study of Curtis's novel. By the way, you may want to inform the parent that the novel isn't about the Civil Rights Movement. The bombing of the Sixteenth Street Baptist Church in Birmingham, AL, is a pivotal event in the novel, but the book is really about the relationship between two brothers and their journey toward brotherly love. If your school doesn't have guidelines for selecting books for classroom study, check out sample guidelines offered by the National Council of Teachers of English.

ဏ ◎ ଔ

**The students in my middle school were abuzz with the gory details of** *The Hunger Games* **movie. The faculty was appalled when the principal, acting on a complaint from one influential parent, made an announcement that students weren't allowed to talk about the movie in school. He even threatened them with detention if they disobeyed. I'm worried that the same thing will happen with the film** *Catching Fire*. *February 2014*

You don't accomplish anything by silencing students. The principal is on the road to creating the same environment that can be found in Suzanne Collins's novels. Suggest that faculty and students approach the principal with ideas about ways to encourage conversation about the books and the films. Launch an essay contest, or sponsor a panel discussion that compares them. Engage parents by asking them to read the books, see the adaptations, and participate in small group discussions with kids. It never hurts for parents and students to engage in an intellectual exchange of ideas. Once children are viewed as people who can actually think and express themselves, the principal may not be so quick to succumb to the views of one parent.

ဆာ ◎ ର

**In addition to reading your column, what's the best way to keep up with news about censorship?** *November 2012*
Start by checking out the American Library Association's (ALA) Office for Intellectual Freedom which maintains a database of challenges to library materials. These challenges are reported in its Intellectual Freedom Newsletter unless the person reporting the challenge asks ALA to keep the information confidential. Another helpful resource is Robert P. Doyle's *Banned Books: Challenging Our Freedom to Read* (ALA, 2010). The National Coalition Against Censorship records censorship cases on its website and in a newsletter that's available for those on its mailing list. You might also want to check the state chapters of the American Civil Liberties Union (ACLU) and the National Council of Teachers of English. Visit the First Amendment Center online. If you do a quick Google search, you may be surprised by the amount of censorship cases you'll discover—some of them may even be in your own backyard. (For more information see the Appendices.)

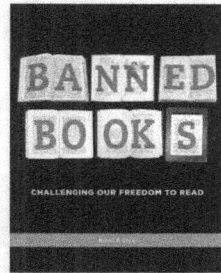

ဆာ ◎ ର

**I really like Lane Smith's It's a Book, and I ordered it for our elementary school library. I wasn't bothered by the word "jackass," which appears in the book, until I saw discussions about it on various online discussion groups. Will I be guilty of censorship if I return the book to the supplier?** *March 2011*
I think you can answer your own question. You don't return a book based on one word and someone else's opinion.

# Appendix A

## "It's About Conversation"

by Pat R. Scales .Originally published in the American Association of School Librarians' (AASL) *Knowledge Quest*, November/December 2007. Reprinted with permission.

My passion for intellectual freedom began at home, not at school. Frankly I don't think that I ever had a teacher or a librarian who really wanted to know what I thought about a work of literature. But I had a father who not only wanted to know my thoughts, but wanted to challenge me intellectually by giving me the books that he read. These novels were by John Steinbeck, Erskine Caldwell, J. D. Salinger, Carson McCullers, and numerous other writers that have been censored. It never dawned on my father that I wasn't ready to read these books. He simply wanted to share them, and talk about them with me.

We talked about the conflict in *The Catcher in the Rye*, and how Holden Caulfield grew. We discussed his alienation and fear and his thoughts regarding the phoniness of the adults in his life. We compared Caulfield's fears to those of Frankie Addams in Carson McCullers' *The Member of the Wedding*. We related their feelings to those of most adolescents. We discussed the term "coming of age," and talked about the journeys of both of these characters. Why did Frankie Addams think that changing her name would make things different for her? At what point did Holden Caulfield realize that he had the same faults that he saw in others? Scenes and words weren't censored; they were a natural part of our discussion.

This experience led me to develop a program at Greenville Middle School in the mid-1970s called "Communicate through Literature." Fifty parents gathered in the school library once a month to learn about the books their young adolescents were reading and to develop skills for discussing the books with their children. No one seemed to shy away from the issues. In fact, the books provided a bridge that allowed them to deal with such tough issues as suicide, teenage sexuality, death, bullying, and drug and alcohol abuse. Before long, parents and students were reading together. Then Judy Blume read about the program and contacted me. She is the person who helped me see how this program actually promoted the principles of intellectual freedom.

I had never thought too much about censorship until I met Judy Blume. It wasn't a part of my life. When I came to Greenville Middle School, *Are You There God?*

*It's Me Margaret*, one of the most censored books at the time, had been out for two years. There wasn't a single copy in the school. I bought five copies for the library, and sold 150 copies in the school book fair in one afternoon. Kids were reading it. Parents were reading it. And while the book was being tried in major newspapers all across the nation, my students and their parents were discussing it together. Censors fear the unknown, often reacting to what the media has told them. My community's parents didn't react to *Margaret* because they knew the book and had used it to spark open and honest conversation with their young adolescents about a difficult topic. Before I realized it, I became a spokesperson for intellectual freedom and, in a proactive way, I began fighting the censorship wars across the nation. By my side were Judy Blume, many of her young fans, and their parents.

The students in my school began to feel special because they were openly reading books that students in other schools in our city, and across the nation, didn't have access to. When a parent at another middle school in our district challenged *One Fat Summer* by Robert Lipsyte, my students wrote a letter to the materials review committee explaining why the book was important to them. The book was retained. *My Brother Sam is Dead* by James Lincoln and Christopher Collier was challenged in another school, and my students posed for the newspaper holding the book. Later, an editor of a newsletter in the Midwest wrote that she thought *Shiloh* by Phyllis Reynolds Naylor wasn't an appropriate book for children because Judd Travers, the character who abuses his dog, was too mean. My sixth-grade students became so angered by the editor's remarks that they wrote her letters. She printed all of them, and even admitted that these students helped her see that she was wrong.

Students began bringing me articles from newspapers and magazines about censorship. And I began teaching them about their First Amendment rights. Together, we became advocates for free speech. Students have opinions, and they want to be heard. Often their thoughts and opinions are enlightened. Students will reject what they aren't ready for if they are truly granted the freedom to read. Open and free. That's the kind of library I always wanted to manage, because that's how my father taught me.

I knew, early on, that the key element to an open and free library is trust. I began by getting to know my students as readers. I asked them to tell me what they liked or disliked about a particular novel. I never passed judgment on their thoughts, and I respected their ideas. They could reject books they didn't like. Soon students begin requesting my help each time they wanted a book to read. They would tell me, "You know what I like." (Wouldn't anyone respond this way when they think someone knows them so well that they can point them to just the right book?) I have a favorite quote from Alice in Wonderland: Alice says, "What is the use of a book without pictures and conversation?" I'm on the side of conversation. It is the only way to build a trusting relationship with students and their parents.

Censorship is about control. Intellectual freedom is about respect. Every time we listen to a student's opinion we have practiced and demonstrated the principles of intellectual freedom. Students want a forum where they may speak; the First Amendment grants them that right. Even school boards find it difficult to vote against an articulate student who is brave enough to stand up and fight for a book.

My father is no longer living, and I'm retired now. I will never forget the books he and I shared, and the conversations we had. Judy Blume is still by my side, and so are my students, all grown up now, and some of them are fighting the book banners because they understand what it means to be intellectually free. My passion for intellectual freedom has defined my career, and I will continue to speak out on behalf of students because they deserve it.

# Appendix B

## *Resources on the ALA Bill of Rights*

Public librarians, school librarians, and teachers all need to make themselves aware of the American Library Association's Library Bill of Rights and its many coordinated statements and interpretations.

Fighting censorship and assuring intellectual freedom is a continuous process. Don't wait until a censorship threat or a collection crisis is immanent. Work with your institution's leadership and staff to fully integrate these essential statements and interpretations into library practice. We have included links to the most essential intellectual freedom statements and interpretations here:

**American Library Association (ALA) Library Bill of Rights.**
http://www.ala.org/advocacy/intfreedom/librarybill. Since 1939, this document, modeled on U.S. Bill of Rights, has provided a clear, succinct, statement of the essential , underlying principles of intellectual freedom in libraries. *(Accessed November 2014)*

**Access to Library Resources and Services for Minors.**
http://www.ala.org/advocacy/intfreedom/librarybill/interpretations/access-library-resources-for-minors. This is an essential support for library practitioners and the young people they serve. Particularly important for public librarians. *(Accessed November 2014)*

**Access to Resources and Services in the School Library Media Program: An Interpretation of the Library Bill of Rights.** http://www.ala.org/advocacy/intfreedom/librarybill/interpretations/accessresources. Every school librarian must be familiar with this core intellectual freedom document and know how to promote intellectual freedom and integrate these principles into everyday practice. *(Accessed November 2014)*

**Diversity in Collection Development: An Interpretation of the Library Bill of Rights.** http://www.ala.org/advocacy/intfreedom/librarybill/interpretations/diversitycollection. With the recent, renewed emphasis on developing and promoting diversity in library collections, this statement can provide important support for collections in all library settings. *(Accessed November 2014)*

**Freedom to Read Statement.** http://www.ala.org/advocacy/intfreedom/state-mentspols/freedomreadstatement. Essential. Along with the ALA Library Bill of Rights, this document should be incorporated as part of every school and public library's Materials Selection Policy. *(Accessed November 2014)*

**Labeling and Rating Systems: An Interpretation of the Library Bill of Rights.** http://www.ala.org/advocacy/intfreedom/librarybill/in-terpretations/labelingrating. This interpretation is particularly useful for those being pressured to label library collections by AR categories, age levels, 'books for boys/girls', etc. *(Accessed November 2014)*

**Libraries: An American Value.** http://www.ala.org/advocacy/intfreedom/state-mentspols/librariesamerican. Any librarian who works with elected officials, library boards, or other community stakeholders needs to read, understand, and communicate the values in this advocacy statement. *(Accessed November 2014)*

**Prisoners Right to Read: An Interpretation of the Library Bill of Rights.** http://www.ala.org/advocacy/intfreedom/librarybill/interpretations/prisonersri-ghtoread. The principles in this document are of particular value to librarians and others working with incarcerated youth. *(Accessed November 2014)*

**Restricted Access to Library Materials: An Interpretation of the Library Bill of Rights.** http://www.ala.org/advocacy/intfreedom/librarybill/inter pretations/restrictedaccess. Restricting access is sometimes embraced as an easy 'solution', a simplistic a way to address public concerns or heated controversies around books or library materials somehow deemed 'inappropriate'. This offers firm support for library practitioners. *(Accessed November 2014)*

**LM_NET: Where School Librarians Connect** http://lmnet.wordpress.com/. "LM_NET is the original listserv for the world-wide school library community. LM_NET provides an excellent way to network with other library professionals, connect to new ideas in library practice, seek advice, and ask library related questions." *(Accessed October 2014)*

**Motion Picture Association of America. MPAA Ratings.** http://www.mpaa.org/film-ratings/. "Movie ratings provide parents with advance information about the content of movies to help them determine what's appropriate for their children. After all, parents know best their children's individual sensitivities and sensibilities. Ratings are assigned by a board of parents who consider factors such as violence, sex, language and drug use and then assign a rating they believe the majority of

American parents would give a movie…The ratings system was established by the MPAA in 1968. The Classification & Ratings Administration (CARA) hosts the rating board made up of an independent group of parents. CARA's mission is to provide parents the tools they need to make informed decisions about what their children watch." *(Accessed October 2014)*

**No Age Banding.** http://www.notoagebanding.org. "This website was set up by writers and other professionals who believe that the proposal to put an age-banding figure on books for children is ill-conceived and damaging to the interests of young readers…We are writers, illustrators, librarians, teachers, booksellers, publishers, educationalists, psychologists, parents and grandparents." *(Accessed October 2014)*

**Parents Against Bad Books in Schools.** http://www.pabbis.com/. ""The main purpose of this webpage is to identify some books that might be considered bad and why someone might consider them bad… Since some of the material in these K-12 school books is extremely controversial and many people would consider it objectionable or inappropriate for children", PABBIS has set up an adult content website for the book under discussion. Users must verify that they are 18 years of age or older to enter the site. *(Accessed October 2014)*

**SchoolTube.** http://www.schooltube.com/ "SchoolTube.com is the nation's largest K-12 moderated video sharing platform, specifically designed for students and educators - exclusively endorsed by over twenty national education associations." *(Accessed October 2014)*

# Bibliography

Adams, Helen R. *Protecting Intellectual Freedom and Privacy in Your School Library*. Libraries Unlimited, 2013.

Beckman, Wendy Hart. *Robert Cormier: Banned, Challenged, and Censored*. Enslow, 2008.

Doyle,Robert P. *Banned Books: Challenging Our Freedom to Read* ALA Editions, 2010.

Fletcher-Spear, Kristin & Kelly Tyler. *Intellectual Freedom for Teens: A Practical Guide for Young Adult & School Librarians*. ALA Editions, 2014.

Jonker, Travis, "Travis's Excellent (Ereader) Adventure," *School Library Journal*, September 2012.

Jones, Barbara M. *Protecting Intellectual Freedom in Your Academic Library*. ALA Editions, 2009.

Lent, ReLeah Cossett & Gloria Pipkin. *Keep Them Reading: An Anti-Censorship Handbook for Educators*. Teachers College Press, 2013.

National Council of Teachers of English. *Rationales for Challenged Books*. Prepared by NCTE in Partnership with IRA. Vol. I and II. Compact Disc. Available via the NCTE online store. https://secure.ncte.org/store/rationales-for-challenged-books

Office for Intellectual Freedom (OIF), American Library Association. *Intellectual Freedom Manual*. Eighth Edition. ALA Editions, 2010.

Pinnell-Stephens, June. *Protecting Intellectual Freedom in Your Public Library*. ALA Editions, 2012.

Scales, Pat R. *Books Under Fire: A Hit List of Banned and Challenged Children's Books*. ALA Editions, 2015.

Scales, Pat R. *Protecting Intellectual Freedom in Your School Library*. ALA Editions, 2009.

*True Stories of Censorship Battles in America's Libraries*. Edited by Valerie Nye & Kathy Barco. ALA Editions, 2012.

# Other Recommended Web Resources

**American Civil Liberties Union.** https://www.aclu.org/. This national organization is the self-described "premier defender of the rights enshrined in the U.S. Constitution." The ACLU has nearly 200 staff attorneys, thousands of volunteer attorneys and offices throughout the nation. Key action areas include: the defense of "individual freedoms including speech and religion, a woman's right to choose, the right to due process, citizens' rights to privacy and much more."

**American Library Association, Office of Intellectual Freedom Blog.** http://www.oif.ala.org/oif/ *(Accessed November 2014)*

**American Library Association, Office of Intellectual Freedom, Intellectual Freedom Newsletter** ($50 a year). http://www.ala.org/bbooks/challengedmaterials *(Accessed November 2014)*

**American Library Association. Privacy Tool Kit.** http://www.ala.org/advocacy/privacyconfidentiality/toolkitsprivacy/privacy *(Accessed November 2014)*

**Association for Library Services to Children. American Library Association. Welcome to the Caldecott Medal Home Page.** http://www.ala.org/alsc/awards grants/bookmedia/caldecottmedal/caldecottmedal *(Accessed November 2014)*

**Association for Library Services to Children. American Library Association. Welcome to the Newbery Medal Home Page.** http://www.ala.org/alsc/awardsgrants/bookmedia/newberymedal/newberymedal *(Accessed November 2014)*

**Association for Library Services to Children. American Library Association. Welcome to the Sibert Medal Home Page.** http://www.ala.org/alsc/awards grants/bookmedia/sibertmedal *(Accessed November 2014)*

**Banned Books Week.** http://www.bannedbooksweek.org/. "Banned Books Week is an annual event celebrating the freedom to read. Held during the last week of September, it highlights the value of free and open access to information. Banned Books Week brings together the entire book community—librarians, booksellers, publishers, journalists, teachers, and readers of all types—in shared support of the freedom to seek and to express ideas, even those some consider unorthodox or unpopular." *(Accessed November 2014)*

**Children's Internet Protection Act (CIPA) American Library Association.** http://www.ala.org/advocacy/advleg/federallegislation/cipa. Resources for those with questions about CIPA at their libraries, scholars interested in the legislative history of CIPA, or those interested in the ALA's position on CIPA. *(Accessed November 2014)*

**Children's Internet Protection Act (CIPA).** http://www.fcc.gov/guides/ childrens-internet-protection-act. "The Children's Internet Protection Act (CIPA) was enacted by Congress in 2000 to address concerns about children's access to obscene or harmful content over the Internet. CIPA imposes certain requirements on schools or libraries that receive discounts for Internet access or internal connections through the E-rate program – a program that makes certain communications services and products more affordable for eligible schools and libraries. In early 2001, the FCC issued rules implementing CIPA and provided updates to those rules in 2011." *(Accessed November 2014)*

**Common Core State Standards Initiative.** http://www.corestandards.org/ "This site is the official home of the Common Core State Standards. It is hosted and maintained by the Council of Chief State School Officers (CCSSO) and the National Governors Association Center for Best Practices (NGA Center). It provides parents, educators, policymakers, journalists, and others easy access to the actual standards, as well as supporting information and resources." *(Accessed November 2014)*

**Entertainment Software Rating Board (ESRB).** http://www.esrb.org/ ESRB is "(a) non-profit, self-regulatory body that assigns ratings for video games and apps so parents can make informed choices. The ESRB rating system encompasses guidance about age-appropriateness, content, and interactive elements. As part of its self-regulatory role for the video game industry the ESRB also enforces industry-adopted advertising guidelines and helps ensure responsible web and mobile privacy practices under its Privacy Online program." *(Accessed November 2014)*

**First Amendment Schools.** http://www.firstamendmentschools.org/ This is a "national reform initiative designed to transform how schools teach and practice the rights and responsibilities of citizenship that frame civic life in our democracy." This is also a fine site for those who want to learn more about important legal cases dealing with censorship and schools. Lessons plans and resources abound. Relevant cases include: Board of Education, Island Trees Union Free School District No. 26 v. Pico, 457 U.S. 853 (1982); Hazelwood School District v. Kuhlmeier, 484 U.S. 267 (1988); etc. *(Accessed November 2014)*

**Freedom to Read Foundation.** http://www.ftrf.org/. "The Freedom to Read Foundation (FTRF) is a non-profit legal and educational organization affiliated with the American Library Association. FTRF protects and defends the First Amendment to the Constitution and supports the right of libraries to collect - and individuals to access - information." *(Accessed November 2014)*

**Games and Gaming Roundtable. American Library Association. Will Eisner Graphic Novel Grants for Libraries.** http://www.ala.org/gamert/will-eisner-graphic-novel-grants-libraries. "Two Will Eisner Graphic Novel Grants for Libraries are given annually–the Will Eisner Graphic Novel Growth Grant will provide support to a library that would like to expand its existing graphic novel services and programs and the Will Eisner Graphic Novel Innovation Grant will provides support to a library for the initiation of a graphic novel service, program or initiative. These Grants will support two categorical grants that will encourage public awareness on the rise and importance of graphic literature, sequential art, and comics as a literary medium." *(Accessed November 2014)*

**National Book Awards. National Book Foundation.** http://www.nationalbook.org/. "The mission of the National Book Foundation and the National Book Awards is to celebrate the best of American literature, to expand its audience, and to enhance the cultural value of great writing in America. " The first awards were given in 1950. *(Accessed November 2014)*

**National Coalition Against Censorship (NCAC). The First Amendment in Schools Toolkit.** http://ncac.org/resource/first-amendment-in-schools/ *(Accessed November 2014)*

**National Council of Teachers of English (NCTE) Intellectual Freedom Center.** http://www.ncte.org/action/anti-censorship. *(Accessed November 2014)*

**National Council of Teachers of English (NCTE). The Students' Right to Read.** http://www.ncte.org/positions/statements/righttoreadguideline *(Accessed November 2014)*

**Young Adult Library Services Association (YALSA). American Library Association. Great Graphic Novels for Teens.** http://www.ala.org/yalsa/ggnt YALSA has complied this carefully considered list since 2007. *(Accessed November 2014)*

**Young Adult Library Services Association. American Library Association. Michael L. Printz Award for Excellence in Young Adult Literature.** http://www.ala.org/yalsa/printz *(Accessed November 2014)*

# *Other Websites Referenced in the Text*

**Accelerated Reader.** http://www.renaissance.com/products/accelerated-reader."
AR is a computer program that helps teachers and librarians manage and monitor
children's independent reading practice. Your child picks a book at his own level
and reads it at his own pace. ...AR gives children, teachers, and librarians feedback
based on the quiz results, which the teacher then uses to help your child set goals
and direct ongoing reading practice. Children using AR choose their own books to
read, rather than having one assigned to them." *(Accessed October 2014)*

**Common Sense Media,** https://www.commonsensemedia.org/. "Common
Sense is dedicated to helping kids thrive in a world of media and technology.
We empower parents, teachers, and policymakers by providing unbiased information, trusted advice, and innovative tools to help them harness the power of
media and technology as a positive force in all kids' lives... ...(P)arents, teachers, and policymakers struggle to keep up with the rapidly changing digital
world in which our children live and learn. Now more than ever, they need a
trusted guide to help them navigate a world where change is the only constant."
*(Accessed October 2014)*

**Facts on Fiction.** http://www.factsonfiction.org/ "We are a resource for parents,
teachers and educators so they can determine if a book may be appropriate for a
particular child to read." *(Accessed October 2014)*

**The Lexile Framework for Reading.** https://lexile.com/. "A Lexile measure is a
valuable piece of information about either an individual's reading ability or the dif-
ficulty of a text, like a book or magazine article. The Lexile measure is shown as a
number with an "L" after it — 880L is 880 Lexile." *(Accessed via web October 2014)*

**The Literate Mother.** http://www.TheLiterateMother.org
"At TheLiterateMother.org, our goal is to provide reliable content ratings for
youth and young adult literature. We feel it is important for parents, teachers,
librarians and concerned adults to be informed about the subject matter children encounter in books. Every book posted on our site is personally read and
objectively rated in four categories: language, violence, sexual content and adult
themes." *(Accessed October 2014)*

# Index

# *About the Author*

Pat Scales is a retired middle and high school librarian whose program Communicate Through Literature was featured on the *Today Show* and in various professional journals. She received the ALA/Grolier Award in 1997, and was featured in *Library Journal*'s first issue of *Movers & Shakers: People Who Are Shaping the Future of Libraries* (2002). Ms. Scales has served as chair of the prestigious Newbery, Caldecott, and Wilder Award Committees. She is a past President of the Association of Library Service for Children, a division of the American Library Association. Scales has been actively involved with ALA's Intellectual Freedom Committee for a number of years, is a member of the Freedom to Read Foundation, serves as on the Council of Advisers of the National Coalition Against Censorship, and acts as a spokesperson for first amendment issues as they relate to children and young adults. She is the author of *Teaching Banned Books: Twelve Guides for Young Readers, Protecting Intellectual Freedom in Your School Library* and *Books Under Fire: A Hit List of Banned and Challenged Children's Books*. She writes a bi-monthly column, Scales on Censorship, for *School Library Journal*, curriculum guides on children's and young adult books for a number of publishers, and is a regular contributor to *Book Links* magazine.

www.ingramcontent.com/pod-product-compliance
Lightning Source LLC
Chambersburg PA
CBHW050530270326
41926CB00015B/3147